WARRIOR

One Man's Environmental Crusade

WARRIOR

One Man's Environmental Crusade

Pete Wilkinson
with
Julia Schofield

The Lutterworth Press
Cambridge

The Lutterworth Press
P.O. Box 60
Cambridge
CB1 2NT

British Library Cataloguing in Publication Data:
A catalogue record for this book is available from the British Library

ISBN 0 7188 2910 7

∞ Printed on acid-free and chlorine-free paper

Printed and bound in Great Britain by
St Edmundsbury Press

For my mother, Minnie and my father.

The book is also dedicated to Annette, who bore the brunt of my selfishness and indecision; to Paul Brown, Ken Ballard, Keith Swenson, Sabine Schmidt, Wojtek Moskal, and to the late Gerry Johnson and members of the first overwintering team who never reached their goal; to Pete Bouquet for taking on an awesome task; to John Castle, Nick Hill and Jim Cottier; to Paul Bogart, Hans Guyt, Remi Parmentier, Monika Griefahn, Harald Zindler, Athel von Kurtlitz, Katia Kanas, Louise Trussel and Pat Moore; to Tony Marriner, George Pritchard, Soo Parr, Hilary Ransom, Jon Thomas Welsh, Werner Stache, Maggie McCaw, Marc Defourneaux, Lilian Hansen, Liz Carr, Chris Robinson, Carol Stewart and the late Elaine Shaw; to those whose vision and dedication got Greenpeace up and running in the UK and to those who struggled in the early days; to the very many whose help and support made our tasks possible, and to the countless good friends with whom I shared these incredible adventures; to the late Jim Slater of the Seamen's Union, and to my partner Gaye Jerrom.

CONTENTS

LIST OF ILLUSTRATIONS

PROLOGUE
Rainbow Warrior

She was only a piece of metal crafted in the shape of a ship by workers in Aberdeen who had built hundreds like her before. She was only one of the hundreds of ships which had been tossed like corks on the unforgiving seas around Scotland and Iceland.

She was worth only two million razor blades as scrap after French limpet mines had blasted a 6-foot hole in her side and sent her to the bottom of a wharf in Auckland harbour. There she lay drunkenly askew for six weeks, her spirits rotting along with her timbers, while the world slowly recovered from the shock of the first act of terrorism in New Zealand in modern times.

She was a wreck, an empty shell, after Greenpeace removed her bowels and souvenir hunters had taken what they could from her decks. She was a tomb also for Fernando Pereira. I walked through the companionway as she lay, now righted, alongside the Antarctic expedition vessel m.v. Greenpeace, and the chill of that awful night in July 1985 was very present. The water rushing up from the engine room, the echo of the blast, the heel of the ship, the swirl of the oily water as it clutched at Fernando's legs.

The stunning reality of that night had subsided from the explosion of a punch on the jaw to the dull ache of bereavement. It was time to lay the Warrior in her last resting place. Quietly, she was towed from her position nestled next to her larger and more modern companion, and taken out to Matauri Bay in the north of New Zealand. A small ceremony conducted by the local Maori tribespeople 'lifted the tapu' of the dead and cleansed the ship for burial. Loving hands bedecked her in her funeral regalia. Even as she was towed to the spot where she would be sunk in 70 feet of water, she brazenly sported the flags of protest amid the gay bunting of sailors; a lady of protest to the end.

We saw her from the bridge of the m.v. Greenpeace which had sailed in her wake northwards to witness her burial in the brilliant morning sunlight. Here she came, being towed by a tug at a sedate pace towards the point where she would be sunk. The spot wasn't hard to locate. Over 50

'You can't sink a rainbow'. The Warrior is sunk for a second time in Matauri Bay, New Zealand *(Latham/Greenpeace)*.

vessels of all sizes were milling around, Cannons and Pentaxes at the ready, video cameras whirring with the hum of modernity; the scene reminiscent of a public guillotining. As bow and stern anchors were laid out from the Warrior, she assumed the distinct air of a manacled prisoner. 'You can't sink a rainbow', my lapel-badge told me. I unpinned it and slipped it in my pocket.

Now the water hoses were playing over the Warrior, designed to bring her lower to the point where the holes cut in her hull just above the water line would begin to admit the rush of seawater. She settled imperceptibly lower and lower. Then the rate of descent was noticeable and the vessels round her jockied for position, skippers shouting at each other to make way. The helicopters which clattered above, cameramen hanging James Bond-like from the skids with cameras, shooting the footage which would zap all over the world, brought an air of carnival. It was too late to reiterate the arguments which had gone on in Greenpeace as to the wisdom of this sinking. She was going fast now, the water half-obscuring the words along her hull. Those of us on the deck of m.v. Greenpeace glanced quickly at each other and looked away.

Her decks were awash. Greenpeace stalwarts in inflatable dinghies took comfort in each others' embrace as the Warrior foundered.

But the old lady had a show lined up for us. She wasn't going the way the planners had calculated – sinking horizontally to lie on the sea bed in the attitude she normally assumed when above the waves. An individual to the end, a rebel even in death, she cocked her snoot at the world. Her bow went down and she raised her stern. At the same time, she twisted along her axis. Great plumes of water vapour were forced from her ports and accesses, as she took her final curtsey. Then her bow hit the bottom. Her stern shuddered 30 feet above the water, and she sank gracefully beneath the flat waters of Matuari Bay.

It was unjust, unreal and ignominious. As though with her passing, my world had irrevocably changed. I had lost not only a dear friend, but also an innocence which forced me now to make the transition from the idealism of the 70s into the harsh reality of the 80s. With the Warrior went a wealth of memories of people, campaigns, good times and bad in Iceland, in the Atlantic, in the Irish Sea, in Dublin, in Barrow, in Reykjavík, in El Ferrol, in Cherbourg and countless other ports. But the tears wending their way down my cheeks that blazing December morning were not prompted by those memories, and somewhere inside I was puzzled as to the reason for them. I couldn't be crying for the Rainbow Warrior. After all, she was only a piece of metal.

1. From FoE to Friends

I had the flashiest car in the whole of south London. I changed women and jobs with equal regularity. Some indefinable thing pushed me from day to day through furies and frustrations.

I took to driving lorries for a living. Atlas Express, BRS, Air Filter Supply, Associated Fisheries – big or small. I would drive so that I was always on the move, able to give vent to my depression and passions.

A close friend was institutionalised after cracking up, adding to my sense of confusion. I began to drink alone and became known for a wicked, searing tongue which could strip someone of dignity from 100 yards. I gambled heavily and lived for Friday nights when I would lose or win a month's wages in a few hours. I cursed the whole concrete nightmare in which I was required to live with its petty attitudes, its restrictive rules and its poverty and squalor. I began throwing tantrums wherever I felt it could have the most unsettling impact. My family invited me to functions with trepidation, and friends shunned my company. I would deliberately provoke incidents.

Other friends were going through their own crises in their own ways, but I externalised my anxieties as much as possible. Extroversion was followed by months when I would sit staring at the wall every night until keeling over from exhaustion and booze. I could make no sense of anything around me. I was angry, but didn't know what at. I was hurtful to people, though I loved them with honesty and intensity. The working class boy from Deptford who had made his parents happy by coming through grammar school with flying colours, and had so much going for him, couldn't quite get it together.

What turned out to be my last driving job was with a giant parcel distribution service based in south London, near Rotherhithe Tunnel. I drove a 7-ton, long-wheel base Ford on what was known as 'West End Bulk' – big loads to large West End stores. I was ready-made for the job which entailed a lot of shouting and bawling, parking in places which would annoy other road-users, and occupying the moral high ground with uncooperative recipients of the goods I was delivering.

Finding the buildings to which the goods were consigned was the first hurdle to overcome: the big stores were easy enough, but many of the goods were destined for the rag trade in Great Titchfield Street. Having found the building, the next problem would be to find the right entrance and park up as close as possible, not an easy task on London's busy and narrow streets. Often there was nothing else for it but to stop in the middle of the road to discharge the load, holding up traffic for 20 minutes or longer.

One day I arrived in Hanson Street with a full load of material for a tiny sweat shop operating on the third floor without lifts. The lorry was already creating an obstruction double-parked in the street. I sauntered up the stairs to the guy in charge amid the clattering of 40 sewing machines and showed him the delivery note. He nodded and said, 'Stack them over there,' indicating a space he had cleared. I stared back at him blankly: 'Pardon?' He repeated his instructions. I told him that for me to climb three double flights of stairs 50 times carrying one ton of material would not only take all day but would leave me decidedly tired, probably to the point where I would need a month off work in an iron lung. He was unmoved. 'Bring them up,' he insisted, and walked away to berate some doubtless badly paid, overworked, mother of five.

'Oi!' I shouted. 'You've got a choice and you can make it here and now. Either you get me three people MINIMUM to help, including yourself, or I take the goods back. The only other option I'll give you is I tip them off the tail end of the lorry. You decide and decide now.'

'If you dump them off the tail, I'll not sign for them,' he said.

'So what do you want me to do?' I asked.

'Bring them up!'

There was a deputation waiting for me back at the yard. I stopped less than five yards in front of the knot of people including the deputy manager, and slid from the cab. 'The load's intact, the delivery note and the overalls are on the passenger seat,' I said, 'and send my cards on. Sorry guys. You want it delivered? You go and do it.'

Out of work, I moped around for a few days and then signed on. From curtain salesman, nut and bolt firm manager, labourer, lorry driver to the dole, it had all been a peculiar merry-go-round.

I called an old mate. As we sat swilling beer that evening and bemoaning the plight of people generally, he fished in his inside pocket and extracted a paperback book which he had bought at a motorway stop on the M1 that day.

'Thought you might like to read this, Wilky. It's all about how we're screwing up the planet and making all the critters suffer as a result of our reprehensible ways,' he said with a grin and his tongue firmly in his cheek. I took the book: *The Environmental Handbook. Friends of the Earth.*

Within two days I was a volunteer for the fledgling FoE. Within a week I was hunting down non-returnable bottles in every gutter and dustbin in Covent Garden. I felt I had at last come home.

* * *

Though I was marginally uncomfortable hanging around 'with those jolly nice people who want to save the world', as my Deptford pals scornfully described the budding green movement, I revelled in the cut and thrust of the work. We operated from King Street in Covent Garden, courtesy of the publishing house which had taken a flyer on the *Environmental Handbook*. This area was still, in the early 70s, the centre of the largest fruit and vegetable market in England and sported all the charm, charisma, mess and squalor of Dickensian London. The market began operating in the early hours of the morning and would resemble a battle ground for the best part of the day, only to return to some semblance of normality by mid-afternoon when the streets would be full of discarded and squashed fruit and vegetables through which many, including myself, would sift for a meal.

FoE consisted of three part-timers and a couple of volunteers. My first assignment was to collect 2,000 non-returnable soft drink bottles which we planned to return to Schweppes as a protest against the waste of materials and energy they represented. The tiny office was soon piled high with cardboard boxes containing hundreds of the offending items but it was clear that, despite my efforts and those of others grubbing around in bins for weeks on end, we were destined not to meet our quota. When Graham Searle, the 'boss' about whom I had heard so much, returned from a trip to assess the situation, he was mightily displeased. We had to increase our stash to a respectable quantity. It was not that the bottles were hard to find, rather we had left it too late to collect enough of them. He told us to go out and buy fizzy drinks, transfer the contents to large plastic containers and add the empty bottles to our pile, which we did. The demonstration went ahead successfully. We drank Schweppes soft drinks for months afterwards and kept the secret to ourselves. Graham was an inspiration.

He was a hard taskmaster, but a great orator. He wiped the floor with the opposition, whether it be on the street corner or before the nation on television. He expanded the campaign against non-returnable bottles into a full-blown packaging campaign, attacking the supermarkets for creating the conditions which demanded ever more sophisticated and inappropriate packaging in order to compete for visibility on the shelves, and then not providing a returnable container system. Friends of the Earth suggested a standardisation of glass containers to cut down the range, and soon we were planning another demonstration outside supermarkets in Edgware Road.

To attract the media, we decided to have some protesters dressed up as packaging. Soon three of us were beavering away in a disused warehouse in Covent Garden to make a giant bottle and a giant jar. After fashioning the frame of the bottle with chicken wire, we set about slapping on what must have been a good ton of gooey papier maché. In order to plaster the inside of the frame, we hoisted it a few feet off the ground with a piece of old rope, and I crawled underneath while the other two passed in handfuls of goo. The work completed, I crawled out to look at our handiwork suspended from a beam. As it began to dry it took on the lines of a creditable bottle. Exhilarated after hours of this work, we began playing football with some of the left-over screwed up newspaper. The vibrations we set up on the rickety floorboards caused the rope to unwind. The bottle dropped with a sickly thud, and the papier maché slid slowly off in a sticky avalanche. We began again.

The bottle and jar duly turned up for the demonstration a few weeks later. I had (inevitably) been allocated the job of wearing the bottle. Susi Newborn, another early stalwart for Friends of the Earth, drew the short straw for the jar which she embellished by wearing a snazzy pair of tights. We were an incongruous sight wandering up and down the Edgware Road calling out our muffled clichés of protest, but it did the job and coverage was extensive.

I became the butt of every jibe imaginable from my friends in the pubs of Deptford and began a strange double life. At home I was 'one of the lads', yet at work I began to move in the circles of ecologists, writers and nuclear physicists. It wasn't only in Deptford that I drank, either. Being next door to a 'market bar' at FoE had its advantages: we could indulge our thirsts at strange times. After a football injury my leg was in plaster for some time, necessitating a lift into Covent Garden before the office opened. Before long, I was an established early morning regular, and often got to work nursing a growing hangover. One evening, Graham accidentally locked himself in the office, and had to inch his way along a ledge outside where he joined us in the pub by coming in through an upstairs window. Soon we were laying into the Irish Mist helping him recover from his ordeal, behind doors which had been closed hours since. I woke up in Graham's house feeling like I'd been run over by a steam roller. He was merrily cooking eggs and bacon. He had the constitution of an ox.

Within a year I was employed by FoE at £10 a week. The organisation grew quickly and moved to Poland Street in Soho. My initiation to the world of Fleet Street began during this time, when I met Bryn Jones, then industrial journalist on the Daily Mirror. Through the network of contacts which is inevitably built up within any interest group, Bryn and I gravitated towards one another as kindred spirits. We share the same birthday and our personalities are very similar – fiery, impulsive and impatient of faintheartedness. Through Bryn, I met another Fleet Street hack – John Rawlins – and the three of us, plus others from the more radical element of Friends of the Earth (plus, it must be mentioned, Rawlins' dog) would cut a merry if odd profile in the Old Cheshire Cheese in Fleet Street, where we would regularly quaff quantities of Marston's Pedigree and toss around wild ideas.

Even in those early days, the clashes between Bryn Jones and myself were legendary. As passions rose in parallel to the alcohol level in the blood, we would regularly round on each other to the consternation of other pub customers and, on occasion, to the concern of our colleagues. Yet it was this rubbing of shoulders with journalists in a social atmosphere which enabled me to see the hacks, with whom I would soon be dealing on a day-to-day basis, as harmless and ordinary and who inspired in me no fear. Their support and sympathy was critical to the task of spreading the word.

Through Bryn we launched a series called 'How to Survive in 1975'. The idea was that we would feed Jones the data on environmental issues and how ordinary people could play their part, for him to reproduce in the *Mirror*. Using up some of his waning brownie points with the editor, Jones engineered a big splash for the introductory issue, heralding a 'major series' on such pressing issues as fuel efficiency, food additives and the like. Our 'back to the 50s' approach met with howls of derision and controversy, to the point where the series was quietly dropped. But by then, I had trodden the hallowed halls of the *Mirror*, and had drunk in all the smoky boozers frequented by hacks and was known to many of them. I felt comfortable in their company and they were likewise comfortable in mine, seeing that not all Friends of the Earth wore sandals, and some actually stood their round.

I presumed I would eventually get a campaign to run or even be asked to join the board. I had, I believed, earned my spurs, and some of the ideas I put forward were resulting in considerable goodwill for FoE. We turned a planning-blighted piece of land in The Cut in Waterloo into allotment space for Londoners, and work with trades unions on energy issues promised great things. Yet I felt that as FoE clawed its way up the credibility ladder, my participation was becoming something of an embarrassment to the more academically orientated staff and advisers.

I began to service the rapidly expanding number of local FoE groups around the country, and wrote a column in the *Ecologist* magazine. I wrote the *Campaigner's Manual*, and whilst generally involved in most of the campaigns FoE were engaged in, I never quite seemed to be given responsibility and felt underused after five years with the group. I was also about to marry. I decided I would have to rejoin the real world.

So, for two years, I slogged it out in the service of the Post Office as a counter clerk, firstly at Yeovil in Somerset and then in Essex. My 'career' was littered with rows with management and short-lived rebellions, unable once again, and however hard I tried, to 'toe the line'.

The phone rarely rang at Halstead Post Office: it never rang for me, so I was bemused when the overseer beckoned. A call from Canada. A guy named McTaggart ringing from Vancouver.

'Is this Pete Wilkinson?' came the distant voice.

'Yes. Who's this?'

'My name is David McTaggart and I want to know if you'd care to come and work for Greenpeace.'

Nothing like getting to the point quickly.

'I'm coming to London at the weekend. Can we discuss it?'

'Sure. Call me Saturday and we'll meet.' – 'Are you paying any money?' I asked belatedly.

I took McTaggart to see Millwall play. It was a truly abysmal game. Afterwards, I negotiated that the embryonic Greenpeace would pay me £25 a week and I would find a part-time Post Office job to supplement my income to £50 a week, the barest minimum needed to pay the mortgage and stay alive. I tried to size up this guy. In his mid-forties, his eyes were alight, flickering and sparkling with energy. His face could change in a split second from a decent imitation of a piece of creased brown paper as he laughed, to a stone wall of impenetrability as he made a statement about which there was clearly no debate and which he would invariably end with the words, 'And I am serious!' He outlined his past briefly: Canadian badminton champion, construction company owner, escapee to the sanity of the South Pacific where he sailed his yacht, the Vega, then drifted in the potential fallout area at Muroroa to prevent French nuclear weapons testing. He spoke directly and economically, with an assurance which was infectious. Although I didn't realise it at the time, I was in the company of a visionary. Even as we sat talking in that Deptford pub, his mind was identifying and solving problems that Greenpeace would have to encounter years hence. I smiled at McTaggart for whom I felt an instant and, as it turned out over the years, unshakeable affection. He rose to leave and I grabbed his sleeve.

'Tell me one thing. Why me?'

'Simple. I phoned FoE. Asked them who was the most 'ornery sonofabitch they ever had working for them, and your name kept coming up. I need 'ornery people. See you next week.'

As he swept through the door, I turned my gaze to the dregs of beer in my glass. A grin spread slowly across my face and I began to chuckle. As I stood up to leave, I let out a whoop of exhilaration.

David McTaggart: former Chair, now honourary Chair of Greenpeace International. The man who has probably had the greatest single effect on my life *(Greenpeace)*.

2. Box Office Attraction

The Greenpeace office was located at 47 Whitehall, a stone's throw from the seat of political power in the UK. The four Greenpeace staff I was to join occupied a couple of small, rent-free rooms and used a borrowed phone, thanks to the British Union for the Abolition of Vivisection. I walked up the rickety stairs and peered in. A guy with a mop of long, black hair sat at an antiquated typewriter hitting the keys carefully. This was Alan Thornton, someone who would play an important role in my Greenpeace fortunes, both for good and bad. We shook hands, and he introduced me to Denise Bell who was sitting cross-legged on the floor stuffing envelopes. Denise, and the third member of the team, the effervescent Susi Newborn, were both ex-Friends of the Earth; I was looking at the trio who could, along with McTaggart, lay legitimate claim to having founded Greenpeace in the UK.

While McTaggart was lining up the pioneers of the Greenpeace movement in France and Holland independent of the other national groups, these three stalwarts were carving out a niche for the UK operation. Thornton, veteran of many a Greenpeace action in North America, seal-lover, whale-freak and tireless campaigner for wildlife, had brow-beaten the BBC into screening a film made on the Canadian ice-floes off Newfoundland of the barbarous clubbing to death of 250,000 two-week old seal pups in front of their distressed mothers, for the benefit of the trinkets-and-trivia market. As a result, the trickle of members joining the impoverished Greenpeace UK had grown into a steady stream, while the response to an appeal sent to the Dutch branch of the World Wildlife Fund had, only days before I arrived, floored everyone by bringing a grant to Greenpeace of £38,000 with which to buy a ship to confront Icelandic whaling.

The Sir William Hardy, an ageing side-trawler past her best, had been owned, ironically enough, by the Ministry of Agriculture, Fisheries and Foods and had been used as a research vessel. It was this vessel, now owned by Greenpeace, which a few months later in 1977 lay in King George the Fifth Docks in London, and over which swarmed an army of helpers and volunteers as she underwent the metamorphosis from a rusting heap into the brightly painted vessel which was to carry the Greenpeace message to the four corners of the world.

A strong bond existed between Greenpeace in North America and the indigenous Indian population, one of whose prophesies spoke of the coming of a Rainbow tribe to put the world to rights. There was only one name the Sir William Hardy could possibly have been dubbed: Rainbow Warrior.

As the time approached for the Rainbow Warrior's departure for Iceland to confront the whalers, we moved offices to a few cramped rooms above a sports complex in Colombo Street, just south of Blackfriars Bridge. We were anything but organised, and as people gravitated to the office to help us we attempted to allocate work on a more professional basis. I took on the anti-nuclear work in deference to the experience I had gained at FoE on energy matters, but inevitably, like everyone else, I was caught up in the everyday work and soon became full-time.

The buzz of working for Greenpeace was addictive. As the Rainbow Warrior left, I found myself in London attempting to field the increasing volume of mail which arrived. One of the letters, one fateful morning, drew attention to an impending cull of grey seals in the Orkneys which were being fingered as responsible for declining fish stocks in the area. I placed it in the 'further action' file and concentrated on the immediate problem of the International Whaling Commission meeting in London at which we planned to demonstrate.

As a measure of the freedom I was finding in Greenpeace (as opposed to the claustrophobia of Friends of the Earth – not to mention the Post Office), I had found myself not only in charge of the anti-nuclear campaigns, but also being canvassed for ideas as to tactics on other campaigns. I had suggested an orderly invasion of the International Whaling Commission during the opening session at which the world's media would be present. We quickly planned the event. Anyone watching from adjoining offices must have thought us quite mad as, time after time, we went through the motions of presenting bouquets of flowers or scrolls of condemnation to non existent delegates, running up imaginary staircases, calling out times to each other and making speeches to the wall.

On the appointed day, fifteen of us made our way to the plush London hotel which was to host the meeting. Smartly dressed, we had no trouble in getting through the security cordon, thanks largely to the mock IWC delegates' badges which graphic designer Reg Boorer had produced for us, bearing the names of fictitious magazines and journals. McTaggart had hired a room into which we crowded while McTaggart himself, somehow an accredited delegate, made his way down into the meeting room to determine the best time for us to make our move.

After an anxious 30 minutes, during which so many cigarettes were smoked that it was hard to see across the room, McTaggart burst in and said, 'Go!' In the manner we had practised so often in the office, we filed towards the fire escape, walked quietly and quickly down two flights and

International Whaling Commission invasion: mustachioed Alan Thornton (left) and Lou Gasparro (right) flank Pete Wilkinson during the peaceful demonstration at the IWC meeting in London, 1978 *(McTaggart/Greenpeace).*

stood before the door beyond which we knew the world's press were assembled together with those in whose hands were entrusted the fate of the whales. I silently prayed that the door was not locked, glanced behind to ensure we were all in readiness and pushed the door open. Shielding my eyes from the glare of the TV cameras, I walked towards the top table behind which sat Ray Gamble, Chairman of the IWC, and his committee.

I walked directly up to him, dodging camera crews who were now panning around to film this invasion. I announced that this was a peaceful Greenpeace demonstration and that we were taking over the meeting. I expected an outburst, but he merely shrugged and said, 'The floor's yours.'

I delivered a speech to a hushed ensemble, attacking the IWC as a toothless and pusilanimous organisation which presided over the passing of the whales while hiding behind the pretext of international concern. As each country was mentioned in turn, their delegate was either handed a huge bouquet of flowers if their record on conservation measures had been good, or a scroll stating 'For Crimes Against Nature You Stand Condemned' if the country had argued for increased catches based on spurious scientific evidence to support their whaling industries.

The ceremony completed, I declared an indefinite moratorium on whaling, as decreed by international public opinion, wished the delegates a safe journey home and closed the meeting. We ended with a two-minute silence for the whales, at the end of which, as we rose to leave, the room erupted in spontaneous applause. Everything had been captured on film and would undoubtedly make the news.

I heard a rumpus behind me. Someone from another environmental organisation had produced a bottle of red ink and, unable to contain his anger as he walked behind the Japanese delegation, had tipped the contents over the head of the delegate, prompting two sumo wrestler look-alike bodyguards to grab him. Uproar ensued. I entered the fray and was pushed and buffeted from side to side, amazed to see McTaggart in the thick of it wresting the protester from the grip of the bodyguards while talking in a mixture of languages he was making up on the spot.

Somehow, McTaggart spirited him out of the building and away. His versatility was impressive, but there was nothing he could do, sadly, about the coverage that evening and the following day. No reference was made to the peaceful demonstration. The incident of ink-throwing dominated the news and cast us, not for the last time, in the role of unruly hooligans.

The Icelandic whaling trip made by the Rainbow Warrior was immensely successful and Greenpeace grew in notoriety. It was clear that we would have to examine, however distasteful the task, our structure and constitution. Greenpeace UK had originally been an 'off the shelf' company, bought for £100. Two existing shares had been transferred to McTaggart and Thornton and later two more were issued, one to Denise Bell and one to me when I became a director in 1978. Despite our attempts to set Greenpeace up in a more structured manner, we conducted business in an entirely ad hoc fashion. Our bemused accountant called into the office one day, and Denise, who had volunteered responsibility for the books, handed over two shoe boxes from a corner of the floor, overflowing with papers, receipts, invoices and all the dross associated with running a business. We were simply too busy and too preoccupied with campaigning to find administrative matters very important.

It was the same with the share issue. Not until years later were our errant ways to wing their way full circle and hit us firmly in the neck. When Greenpeace had grown to be a sought-after prize, control of the organisation was to preoccupy the time of many people. It was an issue which rent huge divisions in the organisation and which almost brought about its demise. It also pushed McTaggart into the unenviable position of taking sides in the fight for control of Greenpeace in the UK, and was to haunt my dealings with Greenpeace for years to come. Not surprising then, that when he asked if I would join the board and become a shareholder and I flippantly replied that it made no difference to me, McTaggart turned his steely gaze towards me with the words: 'You bet your sweet ass it will.'

And the 'Further Action' file was filling up. The Orkney seal cull was planned for November 1978. Falling fish catches and damage to salmon had prompted Scottish fishing interests to demand action from the government. In typical Whitehall fashion, a politically expedient response had been cobbled together: reduce the seal numbers by half. So much easier than dealing with the root cause of the problem, which was Soviet factory fleets literally hoovering the fish from the sea.

Greenpeace officially objected to the plan and the Rainbow Warrior was again despatched, this time to the Orkneys. She would act as a shadow to the Norwegian vessel, the Kvitungen, which would carry marksmen to the islands where the slaughter was to take place. Once on the islands, our protesters would physically protect the seals by standing between them and the hunters.

Initially, the Warrior's presence in the Orkneys prompted only mild interest from the press. But, intuitive as ever, McTaggart predicted this would soon break into a major international story, and I was summoned from London to deal with land-based co-ordination of the coming fracas.

The Kirkwall Hotel was deserted as I checked in. McTaggart was right: within three days, not one room was available and some members of the press were sleeping in tents on the beach, presumably attracted by the prospect of a dead protester lying in front of a living seal with a smoking gun in the foreground.

The impending cull became a front-page story. Children as young as ten left home to hitchhike to Orkney to help save the seals. American, Scandinavian, German and even Japanese film crews swarmed all over Kirkwall, hiring anything that floated or flew. Being the only Greenpeace spokesperson they could talk to without using a radio-telephone, I was wheeled before microphones and cameras at every turn. I began to lock my hotel door at night to prevent the press barging in.

After ten days of coverage, when the story had made the front pages of most nationals at least once, the Department of Agriculture and Fisheries for Scotland called a routine press briefing. Unusually, they forbade me to attend. I was sitting in the bar pondering the reason for the secrecy when, after only a few minutes, the doors to the conference room flew open, to spill out an army of journalists rushing for the telephones. I was surrounded by a mob of interviewers demanding my reactions to the news that the cull had been called off.

It was an hour before I could wrestle free to find a phone and call the ship. Unaware of what was happening on shore, the Warrior had stuck to its task of dogging the Kvitungen's every move, and was by now well out into the North Sea, tailing a ship that was heading home. When the Warrior finally arrived back in Kirkwall around midnight, the scenes of celebration were overwhelming.

Jim Callaghan, then Prime Minister, had received 18,000 letters of protest in one postbag. Greenpeace and the Rainbow Warrior had focused international attention on an act of unjustifiable ecological vandalism, and forced a government climb-down.

It was one of the turning points in the history of Greenpeace and ensured that in future, whatever we did, the press would follow. As one journalist was later to put it, Greenpeace were 'box office.'

At 2am that morning, I was sitting in the bar with friends and journalists when Joe Palin from Radio 4 asked for one final interview to wrap up the story. I smiled at him with half-closed eyelids: 'You've gorra be jokin', Joe,' I said, 'I'm pissed.' We went to his room and did the interview anyway. It was broadcast the following morning, much to my consternation. At the end of the broadcast, the anchorman at Broadcasting House said, 'Pete Wilkinson there, speaking about the decision of the government to call off the Orkney seal cull, obviously elated and slightly inebriated. And who can blame him?'

3. Instant Experts

Relatively stable uranium enters a nuclear reactor and emerges as spent fuel, a highly volatile, radioactive material. It is as though a malevolence, dormant in the uranium for millennia, has been unleashed by the Faustian antics of humankind in its search for endless energy; antics which deny the natural law which dictates that for every gain, there is a loss. By unlocking the Pandora's Box of nuclear energy, homo nuclear has bequeathed to the world a disease from which it will never recover.

The civil nuclear programme in the UK was developed as an offshoot of the effort to develop nuclear weapons. The first reactors in the UK, the twin magnox stations at Calder Hall in Cumbria, went into operation for the express purpose of producing plutonium for the weapons industry, and the fiction of cheap electricity was delivered to placate the British public. The link remains today. So great is the overcapacity of the British electricity generating supply that if all the magnox power stations in the UK were to disappear overnight, the public would notice no difference. The entire ageing magnox station complex generates no more electricity than three large coal-fired stations, yet the nuclear industry receives a subsidy of £1.3bn each year. The question is not, can the world can live without nuclear power; the question is, can the world live with it?

If you want to produce fissionable plutonium for weapons you must first have access to a highly complex reprocessing plant, such as the one at Sellafield (formerly Windscale.) Here, spent fuel rods are imported from around the world, and the plutonium is separated. The remaining radioactive stream is filtered and then siphoned off into the sea through a pipeline, still containing highly carcinogenic elements.

Solid waste, such as spent fuel cladding, and any contaminated clothing, tools and equipment are packaged and dealt with separately. In 1949, a ship sailed from the UK coast carrying a small quantity of solid radioactive waste which was unceremoniously dumped overboard. It was the first recorded nuclear waste disposal, and was to dictate the pattern of nuclear 'waste management' for the next 36 years. Contemporary scientific opinion at the time held that the amount of radioactivity being disposed of was so small, that it would result in the raising of natural radioactivity levels so imperceptibly, as to make not a jot of difference. The esteemed scientists of the day, paid by the nuclear industry, argued that the radioactivity would be dispersed in the vastness of the Atlantic and would, to all intents and purposes, disappear.

Time passed, and the practice continued. By the mid 60s, the tonnages of waste being dumped had risen, and other nations were following the British lead in 'waste management technology' – chucking radioactive garbage over the side of a ship. By the late 70s, the UK was disposing of 1,500 tons of waste a year, though other dumpers had pulled out due to mounting uncertainty as to the wisdom of the practice.

In 1978, the Rainbow Warrior was steaming from Iceland to Spain to continue her highly successful anti-whaling campaigns. On studying the charts, we noticed that the route to be taken by the Warrior traversed an area of the North Atlantic marked as 'dumping ground'. The very site of the UK's radioactive waste disposal activities lay in her path. Hurried research in the office confirmed that a dump would be taking place when the Warrior arrived in the area; too good an opportunity to miss. It was time to become instant experts on radioactive waste. I began the task of digging into the sordid past of the UK's 'radioactive waste management' history, a policy which could be summed up in three words – 'chuck it away' – while the Warrior moved unerringly towards a confrontation which would set Greenpeace off on a course which would see them fined, imprisoned, rammed at sea and bombarded with radioactive waste canisters.

With the Rainbow Warrior on its way to the dumping ground, I hurried to the port of Sharpness in the Bristol Channel where the loading of the UK's waste was being carried out. Without too much trouble, Greenpeace cameraman Tony Marriner was allowed on board the Gem, a 250-foot general cargo vessel chartered to the UK Atomic Energy Authority. After filming, we wandered around the dock watching the loading, chatting to the men. One told us, 'Those big containers hold spent nuclear fuel rods from submarines.' Two large, yellow containers were being secured to the deck, and indeed looked quite different from the regular barrels being loaded into the holds. Had they indeed contained spent fuel rods, the UK would have been in breach of the London Dumping Convention, according to which only low-level waste could be dumped at sea. On enquiring of the UKAEA, we were told these particular barrels were the equivalent of no more than 'a lot of luminous dials from wristwatches.'

The Gem set sail after being loaded with 1,800 tonnes of waste destined for the bottom of the Atlantic. The Warrior was scheduled to arrive a day later. The Achilles Heel of the nuclear industry was staring us in the face. The moral case was overwhelming: why should a small nation assume the right to use international waters as their own private rubbish bin?

But it wasn't only the moral case we were sure of. Our research uncovered details of the US experience. Investigation of disposal operations in California had shown that the concentration of radioactivity on the sea bed was sometimes up to 25,000 times higher than normal; transfer to the human food chain was inevitable. Twenty-five per cent of the barrels known to have been dumped had disappeared. Unforeseen pathways existed through which radioactivity could be concentrated; violent undersea storms took place and, despite the robust nature of the barrels in which the waste was contained, under huge pressure from the deep waters of the Atlantic the barrels could theoretically implode. The original 'back-of-a-fag-packet' calculations, used to justify the disposal programme in the late 40s, were valueless.

As the Warrior ploughed her way southwestwards to the dumping ground, a holiday atmosphere prevailed on board. The July sun beat down, and the sea undulated gently. Crew and media-people littered the boat-deck in various states of undress. Sun-tan oil was much in evidence. On the evening of the fifth day, we entered the dumping ground, and skipper John Castle, a slow-talking, barrel-chested Guernseyman, took the binoculars from his eyes and moved to the radar screen.

'There's a lot of little fishing boats out here, Wilks.'

'I'll get the TV crew jacked up, John. They may want interviews.'

Sure enough, 25 Spanish boats were busy in their traditional waters, unaware that this was now nuclear dumping territory and quite oblivious of the dump which was going on while they were at work; until we told them. Their outrage was duly recorded on film.

In the failing light, John Castle found the Gem, and we closed to within three hundred yards to keep station for the night. At the planning meeting in the Rainbow Warrior's crowded galley that night, we picked on the dinghy crews for the action in the morning. I outlined the plans, and did not hide the fact that we might be risking our lives keeping the dinghies under the platforms from which three-ton barrels of waste would be rolled. Chris Robinson, a phlegmatic, broad-shouldered Australian and probably the best driver we had in the organisation, would be the one into whose hands I would commit my life.

I couldn't sleep that night. Getting up and wandering into the galley at 3am I found most of the others, sipping beer, telling yarns and generally trying to shrug off the anxiety we all felt. We finally slept to wake to a fine, clear day, the sea a shining steel mantle reflecting the golden rays of the early morning sun. If you had to choose a day to go, this was it.

At 7.30 I called the Gem and asked if they would stop their planned operation. I got a curt reply from the skipper, so I asked to speak to the National Union of Seamen representative. He eventually came on the line, having been called away from breakfast. His 'Go to Hell!' was emphatic. I advised the skipper that we would be arriving in dinghies shortly, to peacefully interfere with the operation. He grunted and went off the air.

The 28-foot inflatable was already launched when I came on deck. In it was a Thames TV crew littered with microphone booms and cameras, shouting last positions and timing amid the confusion and noise, as the smaller craft we ourselves would use were launched. Before I realised it, we were underway at full speed, and the Gem was steaming too.

Her passage through the water kicked up a sizeable bow wave in the calm waters, while from each of the two platforms along her starboard side, two high-pressure hoses started to play water in a criss-cross pattern. In order to station ourselves beneath the tipping platforms, we would have to penetrate this wall of water, only then to face the barrels. We careered across the glassy sea and without a pause Chris took us through the torrent of water created by the hoses and slammed the dinghy hard up against the hull of the Gem, directly beneath the tipping platform. It was pandemonium.

The engine of our inflatable roared as Chris held the throttle open to maintain position. Water from the hoses was now directed straight at us, threatening to knock a head off or to bore a hole in someone's back as the gleeful seamen holding the hoses warmed to their task of 'repelling boarders'. Our inflatable bucked wildly as it wrestled with the Gem's bow wave and I hit my forehead on the metal bar across the bow of our dinghy as it rose unexpectedly to a steep wave.

Gotcha! A Greenpeace protester's head is the target of the seamen defending their right to pollute international waters with radioactive waste (*Gleizes/Greenpeace*).

Above it all, the throb of the Gem's engines and the clanking of the derricks as the barrels were lifted from the bowels of the ship on to the platform added to the cacophony of noise and confusion. I glanced aft to Chris's position. As the dinghy rose on a wave, we were level with the gunwale of the Gem and, to my dismay, Chris was taking advantage of these moments to carry out an ungentlemanly conversation with our tormentors. Hanging on for grim death, I restricted myself to the odd emphatic curse, only to find that whenever I opened my mouth it filled with water.

After what seemed an eternity, the dinghy became awash and the weight of water proved too great for the Mercury engine. We dropped back, unable to power away from the ship's hull. We were swept in beneath the stern and watched open-mouthed as the turbulence from the Gem's propeller cut a great swathe through the water only feet from us. As we had dropped out, so the next inflatable, keeping station alongside the action, swept in to take our place and, in its turn, suffer the baptism of water we had just been through. Our job now was to free our craft of water and take our turn as the stand-by dinghy. I looked at Chris. Exhausted, drenched, buffeted and bruised, we grinned at each other from ear to ear.

'The bastards haven't dumped one yet, Wilks!'

'I know! Once more to the breach, dear boy!'

The dinghies could only stay on station a matter of minutes, and before long Jon Welsh's dinghy dropped back and it was our turn to go in again. To our horror we saw that once his dinghy was a fraction off station, a white-clad figure on the Gem's deck pushed a barrel over, narrowly missing our colleagues. Great plumes of water erupted directly in front of the inflatable, threatening to capsize it. As they fell back, in we went again. Another barrel was hoisted onto the platform just as Chris again slammed the dinghy against the hull.

The figure on the Gem leaned over the gunwale and screamed, 'There's only two wooden chocks holding this, and it's coming over, so get out the way!'

I glanced up. The barrel looked menacing as it lay askew on the platform, two puny wooden wedges between us and oblivion. As the Gem rolled on the swell, the barrel rocked in our direction, restrained only by the chocks. The man removed a chock. The barrel slewed alarmingly, jamming itself against the metal lip of the tipping platform. I said a quick prayer and Chris opened the throttle just a little more to keep pace with the ship, cleaving through the water at 13 knots. This was not funny. As the dinghy began to fill with water, Chris had to fight harder and harder to keep us on station. I braced my back, expecting to feel the crushing weight of the barrel any second. The man on deck kept up a screaming monologue, interspersed with Chris's snatched profanities. Momentarily the engine died on us causing us to drop back no more than a few feet. On the Gem the man hit the remaining chock with a mallet, sending it spinning into the sea. The barrel crashed down in front of us, forcing the dinghy to rear vertically before plunging down again in a turmoil of spray and water.

The entire action against the Gem had lasted no more than two hours, but it seemed to us that it had gone on all day. We could do no more. Exhausted, we brought our fragile dinghies back to the sanctity of the Rainbow Warrior. As we forced steaming coffee between parched lips, a crew member commented: 'We took peaceful direct action to the limit today. The next step could only be called violence.'

But the film was in the can. Photos were developed on board. Reports from the journalists were filed across the miles to where eager editors were preparing headlines about the 'New Battle for the Atlantic'. For years, Greenpeace made use of the outrage expressed all over the world at the scenes witnessed on TV screens during the days following that action. And harder actions were to follow.

Every year, the public watched with bated breath to see how the next round in the 'Battle for the Atlantic' would unfold. In 1982, Greenpeace protesters boarded the Gem and chained themselves to the tipping platforms. The same year, a Belgian ship was boarded, and the cranes used to haul the barrels from the holds were occupied, forcing the courts to threaten Greenpeace with legal action. People saw the Dutchman Gyjs Thieme catapulted into the sea when a falling barrel up-ended the inflatable he was driving. The concussion he sustained and the image of his wrecked inflatable shocked people into the realisation that nuclear authorities were determined to be rid of their embarrassing waste. They were sweeping their rubbish under the carpet of the Atlantic and pouring the liquid waste from Sellafield into the Irish Sea.

But as the 70s turned into the 80s, the tide of public opinion was only beginning to turn in our favour. It was time to tighten the screw.

4. Tightening the Screw

Every consignment of spent nuclear fuel arriving in Barrow in Furness, the service port for the reprocessing plant at Sellafield, contains more radioactivity than the bomb which destroyed Hiroshima.

If an accident or fire occurred on one of the ships bringing spent rods into Barrow the entire population would need to be evacuated. This would be impossible in the time available.

The long campaign against what was then called Windscale began in 1981 when, one windswept, bitterly cold November night, I struggled into Barrow an hour late for a public meeting after being stranded on the motorway. I was now Chair of Greenpeace UK, and was to address the meeting along with Peter Taylor of the Political Ecology Research Group (PERG) an accomplished and respected scientist. I suspected the meeting, on this freezing night, might well be over already by the time I found the hall.

On the contrary: it was packed. At least a hundred people crowded outside unable to find a seat. After the speeches had been heard, the questions, accusations, recriminations and pent-up frustrations of these people came gushing out in faltering but nonetheless passionate monologues. We had tapped a deep well of anger. Evacuation plans in the event of a major radiation leak were elementary; fish caught in the Irish Sea could be so deformed they were unsaleable; almost everyone in the town knew someone who was suffering from cancer; the nuclear material on the ships sometimes remained on board for weeks before being taken by rail to Windscale. Hardly surprising that the people of Barrow took Greenpeace to their hearts, and decided to form an action group.

We began to plan a series of direct actions. Initially, we wanted to create the impression that Greenpeace would block the narrow approach channel down which the ships bringing the spent nuclear fuel had to steam. The Rainbow Warrior arrived, and permission to moor was sought from the Harbour Master. He refused, and we were forced to anchor for days on end, almost ten miles from the town itself, outside his jurisdiction. I was constantly shuttled back and forth across these miles by dinghy, to attend meetings in the town, deal with press and then brief the crew who, after weeks of sitting around at sea, were bored and anxious at the delay. The Pacific Fisher – the ship bringing spent fuel all the way from Japan, which we were using as a focus for the actions – refused to make an appearance. A local guy flew his light plane for us out over the Irish Sea to look for her. Still she was not sighted, and the days ticked by into the third week of waiting.

The townsfolk constantly lobbied the Harbour Master to allow Rainbow Warrior into port. He adamantly refused. The skipper, John Castle, and I, after discussion, decided to bring her in briefly anyway without permission, to satisfy public demand. On our arrival the Harbour Master perfunctorily handed John a document stating we would be prosecuted for visiting the harbour. He left to the jeers of the hundreds of people who had arrived to welcome us. We threw the Rainbow Warrior open, and for four hours she crawled with friendly, happy people. Kids swamped the bridge, tugged at the wheel and careered round with gay abandon. As we left to catch the tide the townsfolk of Barrow cheered, and we heard that the Pacific Fisher was due within two days. The long wait was over.

BNFL were aware of the media reports about our plans. They sought, and were granted, a restraining order to prevent us from hindering navigation of any vessel in the confines of the harbour. As we wanted to avoid a charge of irresponsibility, the Rainbow Warrior withdrew, and instead we used the dinghies in a symbolic attempt to prevent the vast ship from entering harbour.

From the water-line her bulk was awesome. She simply ignored our presence, sweeping us aside. We followed her in, and re-positioned our frail little inflatables between her smooth steel hull and the six-foot-wide

Now what? Pete Wilkinson, Bruce Crammond and Susi Newborn among protesters against the arrival of the Pacific Fisher in Barrow *(Gleizes/Greenpeace)*.

A Greenpeace inflatable crushed between the Pacific Fisher's hull and fender, Barrow-in-Furness *(Greenpeace)*.

wooden fenders protecting the quayside. Mooring ropes snaked out way above us.

Townsfolk lined the walls and encouraged us with chants of support. One father, bedecked with banners and carrying his little girl, begged us to allow him to come into one of the dinghies. 'It's her future you're fighting for and I want to be with you!' he shouted amid the chaos.

The Harbour Master paced up and down screaming abuse at us for objecting to the arrival of what Japanese protesters call 'Death Ships'. As the light failed, the crowds increased along the quayside, singing and chanting. Police moved in and the camera crews above us elbowed each other out of the way to get better positions. As the mooring ropes tightened between the quay and the Fisher, she moved inexorably closer to the harbour, a towering wall of metal which could squash us like bugs. Closer and closer she came, and louder and louder we sang.

One of the dinghies began to make that awful moaning sound of a balloon ready to pop. We ended 'We shall not be moved' and changed to the livelier and now more appropriate 'John Brown's Body Lies a Floating'. Suddenly – 'BANG!!' – one of the dinghies' pontoons burst. Then came the repeated sound of tortured rubber and the dinghy I was in was forced upwards out of the water until it squelched on to the top of a fender. We struggled to push it down again, and landed right in front of the Fisher's giant bow. Unhurt, we sped off into the gathering gloom.

We borrowed a wooden launch from sympathisers in the town to replace our own which was damaged, and started again next day at 5am on a low tide. We had planned to make our way stealthily across the harbour before anyone was up, to chain ourselves and our banners to the floating crane used to unload the nuclear waste. In the little flotilla with us were the mums, dads, uncle and aunts of Barrow Action Group, led by their chairman, the irrepressible Terry Smith. Years of rugby playing had bent Terry's nose countless times. He was beside himself with the incongruity of the situation. All my efforts to instil into the event some measure of professionalism – let alone silence – failed miserably.

The rowing was erratic to start with – mostly circular – and the wooden launch we had borrowed began gradually to sink. For every foot of distance the launch gained, a bucket of water came sloshing over the side. The lower it got, the more Terry's jokes flowed. We were weak with laughter as we clambered off the dinghies and over the guardrail; a most unlikely bunch of protestors.

A policeman appeared on the crane deck. His eyes widened at the sight of this rag-tag mob, and he raised his whistle to his lips. Like a rugby full-back he crouched and spread his arms, dodging back and forth trying to catch us all as we made for the stairways onto the superstructure. In the confusion, I managed to tie two banners to the rail before chaining myself to the only cable I could see. Police swarmed over the crane and from below one of the crane workers emerged, hair in disarray, cigarette in mouth, obviously raised unwillingly from his slumber. He eyed me with contempt, spat over the side and then ripped down a banner, tossing it into the water.

He had started on the second one, completed not a week ago on the Warrior, when I called to him: 'Hey, do me a favour, mate. Not that one, OK? A lot of people – some of them just like you – spent days making that banner because they believe in fairness and some sort of future for the kids. Leave it alone, OK?'

He eyed me for a second and then said, 'Aye. OK, mate. I've got the picture,' and walked away.

There were no arrests. The police were tolerant and even, in some cases, sympathetic.

On the way back to London, before I drifted off to the rhythm of the train's clatter, a smile flickered across my lips. Stop them dumping, stop them shipping the stuff to Windscale and – more to the point – stop the reprocessing at Windscale by blocking the pipeline into the Irish Sea. The rest of the nuclear industry would fall like a house of cards. Easy!

Every bone in my body ached, and my ribs were tender. But not from the knocks and bruises; from the laughter and humanity with which people seemed to welcome Greenpeace wherever we went.

5. Rustbucket

Greenpeace were taken to court as a result of the action in Barrow and a permanent injunction was granted, preventing us from ever again going near the port on pain of heavy fines. To my way of thinking, this gave Greenpeace an enormous advantage. I had visions of the entire board of directors being imprisoned as part of a strategy which would further put the nuclear industry on the defensive.

With this in mind, I quietly started looking around for a sacrifice ship. Any old rustbucket would do, the cheaper and nastier the better. Leave it rusty, leave it nasty, paint Greenpeace on the side and take it to Barrow quietly without any publicity, anchor off the approaches and wait for the reaction. The idea filled me with excitement and began to occupy my every moment. Naturally, we could not risk losing the Warrior, but surely we could gladly sacrifice an old vessel which cost next to nothing?

The thought even occurred to me that we could scuttle her in the Barrow approaches to block the arrival of the spent fuel ships good and proper but the pollution which would undoubtedly occur, and the inconvenience to benign shipping in Barrow, sadly, ruled it out.

In 1981 we found a ship in Ipswich with the price tag of £12,000. She was called the Cedarlea. The crank shaft was bent and she overheated. She had for years been gathering rust and a harbour bill, approaching £5,000. I offered £4,000 for the ship and £1,000 for the harbour fees, which was all we had. The offers were accepted hastily.

A week later, six of us climbed on board and prepared to take her to London, though our skipper had sailed nothing bigger than a dinghy. He was however used to a little more equipment. She had no radar or radios, and access to the bridge was via the engine room. As well as the bent crank-shaft and the overheating, the bow was so high that no-one could see over it. The sleeping accommodation was divided by the propeller shaft exactly at head height.

When eventually we were ready to get underway, the skipper rang up dead slow astern and the engineer's telegraph indicated dead slow ahead, so we crunched straight into the quayside. Before we left port, the bill for damage was £800.

The overheating wasn't too bad, and the crankshaft had been sorted out. We bought a VHF radio for £25 – our only piece of equipment on the bridge. With the engineer now responding to every command in reverse, we set out for London hugging the coastline in a drifting fog. At the wheel you could see nothing because of the bow. Neither could you hear instructions shouted by the skipper who had to stand outside on top of the bridge. The engineer fixed a rubber tube through the bridge window and the skipper barked down at us through that. It was just possible to catch what he said by holding the end of the tube firmly inside your ear. In this manner, with me at the wheel, we inched our way through foggy darkness out into the busy shipping lanes of the Thames approaches. The skipper finally decided to anchor when he could see nothing at all. And at that point he noticed the faint glimmer of stern lights belonging to a huge tanker ahead of us.

'Let's give it a try,' he said, picking up the VHF. 'Tanker 300 yards dead ahead, this is the motor vessel Cedarlea bound for King George V Docks, astern of your vessel. The only navigational aids we have on this bridge are six pairs of eyes. Could we follow you upstream please? Over.'

'Cedarlea, Cedarlea, this is the tanker 300 yards ahead of you. Sure, old boy, we'd be delighted. I have you on radar, you should steer. . . .' And that's how the Cederlea steamed for six hours up the Thames in a pea-soup fog to the haven of the King George V dock. For £5,000 we had a ship we could be proud of. She became known throughout the organisation as 'Wilkinson's Folly'.

Nonetheless, it was a sound vessel, and very powerful. Davey Edward, our chief engineer, a small, mercurial Yorkshireman, claimed she was capable of making close to 17 knots, and on one trip he decided to put his claim to the test. As is usual with Davey, I couldn't get a precise time from him as to when the test was to take place, so I more or less forgot about it. Going on watch that night, however, I noticed the sea seemed to be rushing past the hull with greater gusto than usual, and as I traversed the engine room to access the bridge, there was Davey, sitting astride the engine-cowling like a jockey, holding a stick in his right hand with which he urged the engine to greater revolutions, shouting 'G'ern ya bustard! G'ern ya bustard!'

To reinforce his claim, he was found next morning while the ship was still being driven at high revs standing on the bow, his face turned stoically to the wind. Around his neck, he had a scarf, the loose end of which stood stiffly at right angles, trailing away over his shoulder. His twinkling eyes gave him away: he had threaded a stout piece of wire into the scarf to give this 'Biggles' effect. Within minutes the foredeck was strewn with helplessly laughing bodies as one after another came out to see Davey's 'proof' of the speed of the Cedarlea.

She rammed lock gates in Holland, had a near-miss with a cross-Channel ferry, took out several fishing nets off the south coast of England, and caused a derrick to collapse in Liverpool docks as we were lifting an inflatable, nearly gelding mate Dave Greenway.

Despite all this, she was a well-loved ship. Nothing will ever surpass the pride of her crew when, in 1982, a couple of hundred miles south west of Land's End, the Cedarlea and another Greenpeace ship, the Sirius, joined forces to stop the dumping of radioactive waste and were caught in a force 7. The Sirius, an ex-pilot vessel built for shallow water work and reportedly liable to 'roll on wet grass', pitched and rolled heavily in the big seas. The Cedarlea maintained revs and, in a bout of good-natured inter-ship rivalry, ploughed on past the bucketing Sirius, digging her bow deep into a wave and rising majestically to meet the next, water cascading from her decks.

Perhaps it was her popularity among the crew which denied her the fate for which she was intended. After a few months of ownership, it was decided that money should be spent on her, and no matter how much I protested it was clear that the rustbucket was to be endowed with a coat of paint, navigational equipment and other trappings of a conventional Greenpeace vessel – hardly the intention I had had for her.

In 1982 we increased our efforts in the campaign against radioactive discharges from the Windscale pipeline as the next stage in the campaign. We knew our case to be watertight, and had spent considerable energy in commissioning scientific papers which conclusively demonstrated that the discharges from Windscale had the highest radioactive levels of any in the world. There was ten times the national average incidence of childhood leukaemia in the area, and a calculable health impact could be proven. Furthermore, technology existed to cut the discharges to zero.

The task of putting the scientific material together fell to Peter Taylor

The thin green line: Manami Suzuki, Peter Taylor, the author and Chantal Girres appeal for an end to spent fuel shipments from Japan, 1982.

and PERG, whom we had used previously. Peter was growing in stature through his association with Greenpeace, though hanging about with him had its dangers. In Dublin a year or so later he arrived at a press conference as Greenpeace's scientific adviser with his head shaved, and clothed in a one-piece white jump suit. It was a time of 'total cleansing' in his religious calendar and while I naturally respected his religious beliefs, I must admit that I sat in a bar staring into more than one pint grappling with the vagaries of my job. I spread a rumour amongst the press that he had been involved in a car accident and had undergone a head X-ray which required his head to be shaved.

Cedarlea was used in 1983 for the attempt to block the Windscale pipeline, but on the first day's attempt we could not locate the outlet. Quickly realising what we were up to, British Nuclear Fuels took out an injunction overnight preventing 'Agents or servants of Greenpeace' from touching the pipe.

This was an awkward time for us to be faced with the dilemma of whether 'tis nobler to break an injunction or to suffer the slings and arrows of going home defeated. Not only would the bailiffs doubtless invade the London office to sequestrate the assets of the company, but any legal repercussions would also affect Greenpeace International which were that day holding their AGM in Sussex.

I was on board Cedarlea, ready to break the injunction, confident of public support and trying hard to persuade the crew to the same way of thinking. At the same time, I needed to get a decision in favour from both the UK board in London, now chaired by Bryn Jones following the end of my 2-year stint, and from the International board in Sussex. The press with us on the ship followed my every phone call, anxious to have the news before it happened.

The London staff, assuming we would break the injunction, were preparing for a siege. Mike Marmion, a Lancastrian who worked with Film Division, assumed control of turning the office in Graham Street into a fortress. Within hours, there was no possible way of entering except by means of a rope ladder lowered from a first floor window. Inside the building, which had every door and window barred with cross-timbers, the enterprising staff had laid in stores of food. All this was unknown to Bryn Jones, who with Reg Boorer was in court before a judge being warned of the dire consequences of ignoring the injunction.

Bryn and Reg were granted one hour's adjournment in order to consult me on the ship and also to seek guidance from the International Board. They arrived by taxi at the London office with less than 15 minutes in which to carry out the consultations before dashing back to court with the decision. Bryn turned his key in the lock of Graham Street: the door refused to budge. On the entry-phone he was told that the only way in was by rope ladder. He was beside himself with indignation. Someone else came to the upper floor window and they shouted at each other.

'Open the bloody door, man!' Bryn shouted. 'We've got 15 minutes to talk to Pete and International!'

'Sorry, Bryn, you'll have to use the rope ladder. We've barricaded the office,' came the reply from above, with the hint of a snigger.

The neighbours from near-by council flats were hanging from their windows listening avidly.

'Open this door immediately! I'm the Chairman, damn it, and I'm buggered if I'm climbing a rope ladder. Open up and stop being silly.'

'Here comes the ladder Bryn. It's the only way.'

So Bryn and Reg accessed the office via the rope ladder as the neighbours howled with laughter. The staff were helpless too as Bryn, followed by Reg, arrived over the windowsill barking instructions to all and sundry.

Out on Cedarlea I finally persuaded the crew to go for it. To my intense relief Bryn got a decision from International in favour of ignoring the injunction, and immediately phoned the ship to tell me. The press were overjoyed.

Of course, BNFL were there before us. They had welded the pipe so

Greenpeace activists and divers prepare to locate the notorious Windscale pipeline, 70 feet down on the floor of the Irish Sea. Blocking it was to prove impossible *(Grieg/Greenpeace)*.

that our specially designed plugs would not fit. But it didn't matter, the fat was in the fire. We stood in contempt of court, subject to serious fines and possible imprisonment. That was the story, and the press avidly waited to see how heavily the courts would come down on Greenpeace. They didn't have to wait long. The fine was £50,000.

6. Bombshell

During the development of Greenpeace, the task of administering a growing organisation was one which fell – often uncomfortably – on the shoulders of those 'in charge' at any one given time. Originally, the ubiquitous McTaggart would simply make a decision, run it past a few people and implement it.

We stumbled along in this manner for four years but in 1981, as the number of offices in Europe grew, a Council was formed comprising a representative from each of those offices. These representatives, often self-appointed, would meet regularly to discuss co-ordination of campaigns, joint funding of projects, and all other matters which preoccupied the organisation. Fundamental changes were mooted for review, discussion and implementation. Rapidly, articles of association and sets of bye-laws under which the newly emerging structure for Greenpeace would operate were drawn up. The original casual approach to decision-making was over.

A year later, in 1982, the separate Greenpeace entities in the USA and Canada became part of this new organisation. Greenpeace Europe disappeared, and Greenpeace International rose from the ashes. It embraced Greenpeace in New Zealand and Australia too, and fostered a growing number of embryonic groups.

By 1983 we had formed another company, this time a charity, the Greenpeace Environmental Trust, and the International Council had grown in number to nine. I was UK Trustee. The Iran/Iraq war was raging, and the suggestion surfaced that Greenpeace should send its newly-acquired vessel the Sirius into the Gulf. A rapid decision was needed; the vessel was available; the Gulf's wildlife was being decimated by oil spills from crippled pipelines. Here was an opportunity for Greenpeace to move centre stage into an issue which truly combined the two elements of its name. It was a golden opportunity to demonstrate that, whatever the politics of a crisis, it is inevitably the environment upon which we all depend that suffers.

For week after week, the arguments within Greenpeace raged. Some claimed that this was an opportunity, risky to be sure, which Greenpeace would forever rue missing if we didn't act quickly. Others argued with equal passion that to move into this area was irresponsible and outside our scope. Never before had we encountered such a situation and, worse, we could make a great mistake in an area where religious fervour was the prime motivating force behind the conflict.

At the AGM that year, McTaggart used the inability of nine people to come to a swift decision as evidence of the unwieldiness of the structure. With characteristic and necessary disregard for the individuals involved, and his very personal style of chairing meetings, he achieved a mandate to introduce yet another structure which was flexible, strong, democratic and saved a small fortune on international phonecalls and telexes. He established a smaller, more responsive international board of directors. The fate of Greenpeace now rested in the hands of only five people. It was an evolutionary concept. It became possible, for instance, for the Council of Representatives or trustees to fire the International Board which it had elected, should extreme circumstances require it. We became organised in a manner which was the envy of other comparable campaigning groups. From 1981-83 I was a director of both GP UK (having resigned the chair) and GP Europe/International.

Greenpeace began to introduce the same 'state of the art' computer and communications technology as could be found in the offices of Rio Tinto Zinc or ICI. It employed a few hundred people round the world, operated four ships and was reaching the stage where we were all head hunting for staff. Prospective employees of Greenpeace no longer had to have a pedigree of involvement in the movement. If a high-powered lawyer or accountant was known to us, he or she was fair game. The wages we offered at this time were still comparatively small, and few professional people were prepared to take the drop in salary and living standards which accepting a job with Greenpeace normally meant. This was a fundamental dilemma with which Greenpeace is still grappling today. Do you rely on well-meaning, highly motivated people working for an ideal rather than for money? Or do you recognise that the outfit is, to all intents and purposes, a multi-national which needs professional skills at the highest level? I often pondered what is lost and what is gained by the different approaches. Hopefully, we found a compromise, though the financial and ideological gulf which existed for many years between those who were recruited to the offices and those who went to sea for Greenpeace was, to my mind, too wide.

In the early 80s, though, Greenpeace UK seemed forever to be surviving by the skin of its teeth. We had had to pull from the bag one miraculous financial escape after the other, and now our fine for breaking the injunction was crippling. The office at 36 Graham Street was a hive of chaotic activity, but the foundations of the building were literally rotting away. The board of directors consisted at that time of myself, Bryn Jones, Reg Boorer, Tony Marriner (long time employee of the organisation and head of the thriving Film Division), and Mark Glover, a phlegmatic and dedicated campaigner for wildlife. Alan Thornton had long-since resigned, being unable to work under the increasingly restrictive guidelines of peer review and collective approval which we all now had to undergo; though he retained a formal interest in the organisation. None of us possessed, in even the smallest quantity, the management skills necessary to run the office, and the various attempts we made at employing someone to correct our deficiencies all ended in failure. What we did collectively possess, in large amounts, was a flair for actions which put Greenpeace in the press and on TV with clockwork regularity.

It was around this time of gruelling, hand-to-mouth existence that a bombshell hit us. When Alan had walked away from Greenpeace he had bought himself a ship, the Balinoptera, and set off for Norwegian whaling grounds. He had also established the Environmental Investigations Agency to expose the undercover trade in endangered species. But all the time, he was waiting in the wings watching our efforts. Now he called an Extraordinary General Meeting through his lawyer.

He had two shares in the company and on paper held a strong hand. His shares, plus that of Denise Bell, could defeat the two held by myself and McTaggart. I stared bleary-eyed at the notice for the EGM, delivered by registered post. I read and re-read the motions. They proposed removing me from the position of executive director, together with the other board members, and installing Thornton and Bell in charge of Greenpeace UK. I phoned McTaggart.

McTaggart's reaction stunned me. He insisted that the fault lay squarely on my shoulders for not taking sufficient care of the legal minutiae in 1977. I pointed out to him that back then I had not the slightest notion what the purpose of a share was. 'Well you're sure finding out in a hurry now!' he said.

I went to see Thornton in an attempt to reason with him. He was scathing in the intensity of his attack, on me in particular and on Greenpeace UK in general. He found me a 'useless campaigner' and unworthy of the position I held. I was defending my position in the organisation by shoring up the walls of my directorship with the appointment of 'old drinking buddies' to the board. Nothing would placate him, and it seemed as though nothing would avert the coming showdown.

Legal advice gave the board a ray of hope in what now became an embittered struggle. The extra share which Thornton had been issued, the share issued to Denise Bell, and indeed, the one issued to me, had been allocated years ago in ignorance of company law, our lawyer advised us. The only valid shares were the one each which had been originally given to McTaggart and Thornton. They alone stood as the combatants in this fight for control of Greenpeace in the UK.

McTaggart forced a stalemate at the EGM, and Alan and I retired to glare at each other.

As we struggled on with bad tastes filling our mouths in the UK office, we were heartened that the latest newsletter made a clear profit of £3,000, an amount which would see us through the rest of the year having met our financial forecasts. Then the lawyer's bill arrived for advice on the share issue – £3,200. The money we had painstakingly raised from supporters to prevent damage to the environment, paid instead, for an internal battle.

A respite had been attained, but no resolution had been found. Alan wanted me out. Friends and colleagues tried to break the deadlock. He was visited by Remi Parmentier, leader of the French office, and by Hans Guyt from Holland. He wouldn't budge.

Eventually, after weeks of anguish and uncertainty, it was agreed that Greenpeace International would hold both of the legal shares in trust for the UK office. It was a difficult and painful time, and I breathed a huge sigh of relief when McTaggart promised a telex to pass on to Alan confirming the arrangement.

I called Alan and told him the telex would arrive in an hour. He agreed to collect it from the office. Forty-five minutes passed and no telex had arrived.

Throwing caution to the wind, I called the over-worked McTaggart at International headquarters and pleaded with him to send the damn telex! It came through, punctuated with profanities and promising before God, his mother and all that was holy, to honour the agreement. It hardly constituted a legal document. To say it was tongue in cheek would be an understatement.

Thornton was to lodge the telex with his lawyer as proof that the arrangement was bone fide, but I could not possibly hand him this one. Selecting the 'local preparation' mode on the telex machine, I faked a moderately-worded telex and within seconds of ripping the paper bearing the message from the machine, I was handing it to a stony-faced, tight-lipped Alan. He scrutinised it as I held my breath, then spun on his heel and was gone from my life – for the time being.

7. Rubbish without a Bin

Relieved of the threatening black cloud which had hung over the office for what seemed like an eternity, we turned our attention once more to the campaigns in hand.

We raised £38,000 of the Windscale Injunction fine, and the judge waived the remainder, commenting that he was sure 'we were all honourable people.' We had lost a battle but won a resounding victory in the war against the poisoning of the environment around the reprocessing plant on the Cumbrian coast.

The sort of high-profile actions Greenpeace carried out at Windscale were augmented by a series of smaller but equally effective actions. Two such incidents are worth relating, partly as they give an insight into how luck often played a decisive part and partly because they illustrate the way in which Greenpeace was prepared to sail so extraordinarily close to the wind.

We chartered a train to bring 350 protesters from Barrow in Furness to London where they would march from Euston to Downing Street to demand an end to the poisoning of their coastline. Jean Emery, a small bundle of furious energy who had taken over from Terry Smith as leader of the Barrow Action Group, convinced us all that a dustbin of contaminated mud on a trolley at the head of the procession would symbolise the plight of the Cumbrians, living, as they indeed were (and still are), in a nuclear dustbin.

As the procession arrived at Downing Street, a deputation including Jean delivered a letter of protest to number ten. On rejoining the main body of protesters, she up-ended the dustbin, from which flopped a forlorn dollop of mud. As the police closed in and wearily told us to move on, Jean told them that this particular piece of uninviting sludge was contaminated with over 200 radionuclides, one of which was plutonium.

Whitehall was cordoned off. People and traffic were evacuated and the Fire Brigade were called in to deal with it. The press, naturally, gobbled up the story. The point was easy to make: Cumbrians live with this pollution daily; their kids play on beaches contaminated with the stuff; yet a small dollop on the doorstep of the mighty forces the closure of one of London's main thoroughfares and promotes panic.

So successful was the mud-dumping episode, that we decided to repeat it, this time using a larger amount – six tons. I recruited the inexhaustible services of Les Parris, an asphalter, and hired a tipper truck to collect the mud. Shovelling six tons of mud into the back of a lorry was not a viable proposition, so we also hired a mechanical digger for the weekend. Les and his party of helpers from Barrow donned pretend Cumbrian Water Authority smocks to divert attention and set about filling the skip on the back of the lorry. It was covered with plastic to prevent releases of the more dangerous radionuclides on the journey back to London, and on arrival it was hosed constantly to prevent particles from dispersing into the air.

Very early on the Monday morning we set off from the Graham Street office for the Department of the Environment, upon whose steps we intended to dump it. Everyone else would be busy with banners and hoses, and I had the job of actually pulling the lever that would dump the stuff while Les was locked in the cab ready for a quick getaway in the hired lorry. He showed me which lever to pull, and I marked it with tape to avoid making a mistake. Just about every TV company, radio station and newspaper had promised to be there.

I drove in the cab with Les. On the approach to the building he had to make a three-point turn in order to present the rear of the lorry to the steps of the Department. As the press swarmed round, I jumped from the cab, locking in Les as promised, and noticed with horror that the violent motion of the vehicle as Les swung it across the road had disengaged the skip from the tipping lugs. I would have to re-engage the lugs and start the tipping process all over again. To make matters worse, the skip, which Les had lifted from the bed of the lorry earlier, was swinging freely fore and aft. As the cameras whirred and the team of protesters rushed into position, I struggled with several levers, pushing them in all directions in a frantic effort to get the thing under control. Les was leaning out of the cab calling me all the names he could think of; Reg Boorer, holding the end of a banner, was shouting too, the TV guys were shouting, and my ineptitude was threatening to scotch months of planning. I ignored the noise and concentrated. Finally – thankfully – CLUNK – in went the lugs.

'PLEASE, Wilks', screamed Les, 'just pull the one with the tape on NOW!' – six tons of irradiated mud spilt directly over the steps of the DoE – on the button. Hoping to be hoicked away by the police in the middle of a speech to camera, I looked around, but not a solitary policeman was to be seen. I motioned to one of the support people: 'For Christ's sake go and phone the bloody police. Tell them there's a raid on the DoE. Tell them anything but get them here fast!'

Les, assuming as I did that the police would arrive within seconds, had made his getaway with the lorry. In his haste he forgot to retract the jacks at the tail, and the off-side jack bit deep into tarmac, taking out a

Windscale protest: a 6-ton load of contaminated mud from Ravenglass Estuary is tipped onto the steps of the Department of the Environment *(Greenpeace)*.

lump of road. He also knocked a cornice over at the end of a low wall.

Thankfully, a squad car came screaming up, and I heard the familiar words: 'Wilkinson, you're nicked.'

As I sat, still talking to the press through the squad car window, most of my colleagues were arrested too. We sped away to the police station and the Inspector in charge swung round in his seat, winked, and said: 'Great action, guys, a pleasure to do business with Greenpeace. Imaginative, outrageous but always peaceful!"

We were banged up in two cells and told we'd be charged both with disturbing the peace and obstructing a public highway. A solicitor came to take our particulars.

'No previous convictions, I assume,' he asked through the grill in the door.

'Well, actually, I was done years ago for swearing in public,' I offered in a spirit of honesty.

'Oh, really. Well, that should be OK,' he said. 'No-one else?'

'Yes. Me.' This from one of the volunteers I'd never seen before. 'I was convicted of embezzlement.'

'I see,' said the brief, looking more querulous as he noted these facts down.

'And me,' came another voice from an equally unfamiliar face. 'Grievous bodily harm two years ago, but it was a stitch-up.'

The brief could stand it no more. 'This IS the Greenpeace contingency here, is it not? Let's hope that the judge doesn't ask for any previous, I couldn't stand the strain!'

We were fined a total of £40. When Les returned the truck to the hire company the following day, we were in trouble. The irate manager wanted to know how his vehicle had been featured on national television delivering mud from a location 400 miles away, when it had been hired for 'local' work. Typical of Les and his ability to go on the offensive, he dismissed the manager's outrage, saying a late job had come up, and presented him with a receipt for new tyres which he'd had to buy after the police stopped him on the M6 for having bald ones. Les walked out of that hire shop with a significantly reduced bill and a big grin on his face.

In the meantime, the Fire Brigade were called in again to deal with the mud, and handed it over to the UK Atomic Energy Authority. We spent the next several weeks logging the number of places they tried to dispose of it, as one local council after another refused it. Eventually, all six tons were taken back to Cumbria.

The issue of the Windscale discharges reached an international audience, and demands for an end to them were strident and insistent. In the face of this mounting pressure, BNFL reduced its discharge levels significantly, whilst claiming this was part of an on-going clean-up programme.

The Paris Commission, an international body charged with overseeing liquid discharges into European waters, was to sit shortly to consider the overall levels of radioactive waste from reprocessing plants. On the eve of the meeting to be held in Oslo, I repeatedly rang the Department of the Environment offices to ask of William Waldegrave, then Minister for the Environment, how the UK delegation would vote, given that BNFL had agreed to reduce its discharge levels.

I argued that in the light of these reductions, the UK would have no alternative but to vote in favour of the Scandinavian motion introducing the principle of ALATA (as low as *technically* achievable). This was proposed to replace the scandalous ALARA (as low as *reasonably* achievable), which had allowed the UK to justify its high discharge levels for 30 years. Waldegrave prevaricated. I persisted. I told him I had informed the press I was asking for his clarification, and that they too were awaiting a reply. Eventually, he agreed to bike round details of the British vote.

The letter arrived only minutes before I was to rush off to catch the plane to Oslo, and as I grabbed my bag, I tore the envelope open. It said that the UK delegate to the Commission had been instructed to vote in favour of ALATA, the substance of the Scandinavian motion. As such, that tiny scrap of A5 paper was one of the most significant documents to come my way since I began working for the environmental movement. We had forced the UK to accept their responsibilities and we had dragged BNFL screaming to the forum of public accountability.

I met the UK delegate in the lobby of the swish hotel in Oslo the following morning. He slapped me on the back and congratulated Greenpeace for doing such a splendid job in bringing these issues to the attention of the public and to parliament. I thanked him and told him I was glad to hear that he would be voting for the Scandinavian resolution.

'Come now, Peter,' he said patronisingly, 'we won't be going that far! We have to deal with these issues here in a politically sensible manner!'

I took great delight in holding his gaze as I reached into my pocket for Waldegrave's letter.

'Oh but you will be voting for it. Even if you don't know what your instructions are, Greenpeace does!'

I handed him the letter and watched his eyes widen. 'I'll make a copy of it for you if you wish,' I added, but he was off to the phone to confirm the news he had received, to his chagrin, from Greenpeace. We issued a press release: 'UK delegate to the Paris Commission in Oslo receives his instructions from Greenpeace.' Victories are hard enough to come by and I wasn't going to let this pass without milking it for all it was worth. The Greenpeace delegation had a drink or two that night – and then paid for it the rest of the week, so outrageously expensive is Norway, by surviving on peanuts, chocolate and burgers and drinking only when one of the national delegates was paying.

8. Sir John Intervenes

Opposing the nuclear industry had, to this point, been fun indeed, if hard work. Greenpeace were now involved in a series of direct actions all over the world to highlight the fact that nuclear weapons testing – the final and inexcusable piece in the nuclear jigsaw – was in full swing, to the detriment of the environment and the populations who live downwind of the test sites.

As part of Greenpeace UK's campaign we had in mind a protest which we felt would capture the imagination: A banner demanding that it was 'Time to Stop Nuclear Testing' hung from the top of the Big Ben tower, across the clock-face.

During the planning stages, someone walked into the office and handed me a brown envelope, saying, 'This may be of interest to you.' I put it to one side; lots of people dropped things off which turned out to be wild ideas for actions or campaigns.

A couple of hours later, sipping tea, I idly pulled the two sheets of photocopied paper from the envelope. The cup remained an inch from my lips as I read the text.

What I had before me were the highly confidential minutes of a meeting between government departments – including the Ministries of Defence and Environment. They had discussed ways to dispose of radioactive waste from defence sources contaminated with plutonium. This waste was technically classified as 'highly active'.

The minutes revealed a suggestion to package the material in such a way that it would be possible to hoodwink opponents of sea dumping into thinking it was low-level waste. This idea had been dropped, but only because the presence of suspiciously large packages 'might lead to awkward questions'. Ways of circumventing an international agreement had been openly discussed at a very senior level of Government. This was dynamite, and I hastily called a meeting of our own.

We decided to mount a press conference to coincide with The London Dumping Convention. When we held it, 100 press releases disappeared in two minutes. We hit the airwaves in a big way, starting with the Today Programme on Radio Four, interviews all day and on the early evening news, the nine and ten o'clock main slots and the late-night current affairs programmes. Greenpeace received front page coverage, and a raid by Special Branch three days later. As they couldn't trace the identity of the informant from my files, they invited me to Scotland Yard. Under the Official Secrets Act, they pointed out, I was as liable to prosecution as the person who had leaked the minutes. It would help if I co-operated. There was nothing I could tell.

After this, we were careful to feed the press stories we knew would not disappoint them. On planning an action, we would tip off ITN or the BBC to get their cameras to location X at time Y. They had come to trust us and rarely failed to show up. We wouldn't let them down, and they honoured our embargoes.

When we came to carry out the climb on Big Ben a few weeks later, the press were ready, but we walked right into a police trap. They knew of our plans; one public spirited policeman told me in confidence later, 'Just for the record, it wasn't a phone tap – look at your volunteers.' We had been infiltrated as a result of the government leak. Graham Street was usually swamped with people and most plans were discussed openly; we had hectic schedules and open-plan offices – it was unavoidable. We laid down stricter rules for the volunteers and carried on as usual. There was nothing else we could do.

The Big Ben climb was rescheduled. I was uneasy, but went off to Windscale on the Cedarlea content that all necessary plans had been made. On the night before the action, I called the co-ordinator, George Pritchard, from the ship to check that all was in order. A decidedly reticent George stammered into the phone from London.

'L . . . Look, Wilks. I . . . I've had to call it off, mate.'

'Call it off? What the hell for? We've planned this for months!'

He told me a tale which I find hard to repeat even now. Certain, let's say, more ephemeral friends of his participated in an activity which they referred to as 'astral travelling'. During a recent walkabout, presumably among the stars, they had met up with Sir John Betjeman, the late Poet Laureate, who had been dead for a year or more. He had 'told' them that the planned Greenpeace action was 'wrong' at that particular time and he foresaw a catastrophe if it went ahead.

George's friends were convinced of the need to call it off and offered to send George himself on an astral journey. This he had declined. The thought of the portly George roaming around the stars looking for dear old Sir John broke the grim frown which had formed when he told me of the cancellation.

When news of the climb didn't appear in the morning's papers, the inevitable happened: McTaggart rang.

'What in hell is going on in that office? What's all this bullshit?' he roared down the phone. 'You're telling me that an action you've had planned for months, which is part of an International strategy, which has been paid for by International, was called off on the say-so of some guy that's been dead for a year?'

'That's about the strength of it, David,' I replied lamely.

We vowed to have one more attempt. We bought a London double-decker bus and cut a hole in the roof. From the hole, we planned to extend a ladder from the bus to scaffolding which surrounded the clock-tower for renovation. From there the climbers could make their ascent. Security was high around the House of Commons at this time, and I was worried that we'd be confused with the IRA. I thought we had a very slim chance of getting the climbers started before we were arrested.

The day arrived, and at 4am I collected the bus from the warehouse in Dockland where the alterations had been made. As I drove into London, early-morning hopeful passengers shouted abuse as I sped past bus stops. My hands were clammy with sweat. After loading the climbers and UK direct action coordinator Dave Roberts, we set off for Big Ben.

As we approached Westminster Bridge, I slowed to allow a regular London bus to overtake. It would stop at the very point where we needed to park while the climbers made their exit. Creeping over the brow of the bridge, I could see that the bus had deposited its passengers. The stop was clear. This was it – now or never!

I pulled up as casually as possible. It was approaching 6am and a café across the road was just opening up. I heard cursing from the top deck and the scraping of metal against metal as the ladder was pushed through the hole, then the chink of climbing equipment. To my horror, I saw a police car speed round the far side of Parliament Square and career in our direction. But it carried on going, obviously to arrest more dastardly people than us. I held my breath and watched the guys clambering across the ladder to the scaffolding. The café-owner suddenly saw us and started screaming and pointing us out to passers-by. Dave Roberts shouted:

'They're away! GO! GO! GO, Wilks!!' I fumbled the gears and spent more precious seconds locating first.

We lurched forward for the getaway. As we made the circuit of Parliament Square and passed Big Ben again, the climbers were half-way up, mere dots clambering up the scaffolding. We cheered them as we passed and concentrated on securing the bus from arrest. Police ran past round the Square, ignoring us again, whistles blowing, radios crackling. But they were too late. In another minute or two, our climbers would be slung from their harnesses, immovable unless the police wanted to send them crashing to their deaths by cutting the ropes from which they hung.

We parked the bus and made our way back on foot to the scene of the crime. Even from the south side of the bridge, the banner stood out clearly – 'TIME TO STOP NUCLEAR TESTING' – and above it, safely ensconced in their harnesses, dangled two intrepid climbers. It looked very impressive. We called them on the VHF radio and congratulated them.

Nuclear weapons testing protest: climbers scale Big Ben *(Greenpeace)*.

'Great view from up here, you guys,' was their retort.

The police were everywhere. Anyone connected with Greenpeace was arrested and I was asked to bring the climbers down. I refused. Sightseers, tourists, supporters and well-wishers gathered in ever-growing numbers. By 6pm, I was released on the understanding that this time I would call the climbers down, which I did gladly as they had been hanging there for nearly 12 hours. Loud cheers greeted them as they were led exhausted to the police van. They, and the late Poet Laureate, had done us proud.

Offices in France, Germany and Holland were also firing on all cylinders around this time, and the need to deal with foreign press became a daily event. I travelled to Italy, Spain, Holland and even the Soviet Union to speak for Greenpeace. I sailed with Brazilian TV crews and Scandinavian reporters. I was interviewed on every major radio and TV programme in Europe, the USA and Australasia and I loved every minute of it.

The best moment came when BBC2 made a film on the life and times of the organisation. It won the hearts of millions across the country and netted Greenpeace a cool £100,000 in boosted donations and membership.

In the wake of the programme, we were inundated with requests for interviews. A quiet, sincere woman from Radio Four convinced her editor I was 'Any Questions' material. I was more dubious than she was, as my natural confidence seemed to disappear when faced with questions other than those on environmental matters. But she didn't have too hard a job convincing me I could be up there with government ministers and other Oxbridge high flyers. At our third interview, a trial run, I had to comment on stories picked arbitrarily from the *Daily Telegraph*. I breezed my way through four or five topics, putting an environmental spin on every answer, raising the odd laugh now and again and enjoying myself. Then we came to the financial section and a story about the value of the deutschmark against the dollar.

'I don't know anything about economics' I said, 'and who is this Dow Jones anyway?'

The call came next day. She said it was probably not in anyone's interest if I participated. Thus ended my one real chance of making the chatshow merry-go-round and a lucrative second income. I decided then I was not Jonathon Porritt.

9. Outmanouevered

The London Dumping Convention finally outlawed the dumping of low-level radioactive waste at sea, a decision forced by our uncompromising campaign and which came into force in 1985. Political muscle was provided by the Spanish delegation to the Convention. A newly elected government would no longer tolerate dumping in their fishing grounds and they forced the issue to a vote. The Greenpeace delegation sitting at the back of the conference hall held its breath. The vote was carried by 18 to 7.

Flushed with the euphoria of success, we found it hard to take in an immediate statement made by the British. They announced that the vote was 'not legally binding' and therefore they would carry on dumping regardless.

We had been badgering the National Union of Seamen about their involvement in sea-dumping for years. Jim Slater, the General Secretary, was in favour of a withdrawal of labour on the operations, but was hamstrung by his executive committee. We had kept the pressure up and the arguments flowing, with little result.

But when it was confirmed that Britain did indeed intend to defy the vote, I rushed to see Jim at the Seamen's HQ in London.

'It's not a minority Greenpeace issue now,' I told him, 'Your men will have to carry out an operation which is outlawed by international opinion.'

Jim swung into action and called his executive. They were prepared to adopt a policy of non-cooperation, if other transport unions would back them; otherwise, they felt, any action on their part would be ineffective and would isolate the NUS. So we invited representatives of the Transport and General Workers Union, The National Union of Railwaymen and the train-driver's union ASLEF, to attend a Greenpeace briefing.

Before committing themselves to backing industrial action, these unions requested a whole series of papers, looking into alternatives to sea dumping, the present routes used for waste collection, the consequences of a ban, and a long list of other issues. We had a scant three months before the next dump was to take place, and we set to work furiously putting the information together.

With only weeks left, we submitted the papers and sat back. It was a nail-biting time. We learnt that the Atlantic Fisher, the sister ship to the Pacific Fisher, was currently undergoing a face-lift in Barrow to make the dumping operation 'more efficient'. Yes, admitted a spokesperson, the Atlantic Fisher would have the ability to dump its cargo directly through the keel by means of a 'moon-pool' built into the ship.

'Would this be an anti-Greenpeace measure, by any chance?' we asked.

'Oh, no. Just a more efficient manner in which to dump.'

Jim Slater phoned at last.

'Well, Wilkinson, we're all in except the railwaymen. They want time to consider it further. But as far as the other lads are concerned, we've agreed we will not handle radioactive waste destined for the sea. How's that?"

I could have kissed him.

We made Jim our Environmentalist of the Year and presented him with a plaque to commemorate the historic occasion. I was made an honorary member of the National Union of Seamen, along with George Pritchard, another stalwart of our anti-nuclear team. The Atlantic Fisher, with its newly constructed moon-pool which had cost the UK Atomic Energy Authority £500,000, lay idle in Barrow and was eventually released from her contract.

Greenpeace were fêted in Spain. Activists in Holland and Belgium, many of whom had been arrested and treated abysmally during protests in the latter years of the campaign, rejoiced in the decision of the UK trades unions. The ban was endorsed by the British TUC and the International Transport Workers' Federation. It applied in the USA and round the world. We believed then that the dumping of radioactive waste in the deep ocean was finally over, and that the practice would never be revived (we weren't to know that the Soviet Union would be exposed years later for continuing to dump at sea).

It was probably this campaign more than any other which demonstrated our effectiveness. The 'unique alliance' between Greenpeace and the unions (a phrase coined by Jim Slater) was of great concern in political circles. It was one thing to deal with a pressure group, but quite another to deal with the greening of the trades union movement!

Our Big Ben protest had received gratifying publicity, and Rainbow Warrior was continuing the campaign against nuclear weapon testing at the other side of the world, by undertaking a high-profile Pacific Peace Voyage.

Greenpeace had another victory too. After relentless pressure from our members, the EEC banned the importation of Newfoundland baby seal pelts which were made into trivia. We were breaking through the underfunding problem (largely thanks to the BBC 2 documentary) and we met the half-way mark of the eighth decade of the century with a growing belief in an ability to fundamentally change the world for the better.

Ominously for some of us, however, the International secretariat was creating the spectre of the centralisation of Greenpeace. National offices round the world faced the prospect of being reduced to fund-raising typing pools, providing cannon fodder for the direct action required by distant decision-makers, instead of generating their own home-grown campaigns. Another spectre loomed large in my life again, in the shape of Alan Thornton, the resilient Canadian who wouldn't lie down.

For years, McTaggart had moaned at me for appointing what he considered an introverted board to the UK office. The UK board itself was not unresponsive to the criticisms, and had agreed in principle to include external 'worthies' who would add strength, depth and intellect to the numb minds which McTaggart considered were sitting in the boardroom at that time. From a national perspective, the UK board was anything but numb; however, most of the problems we experienced (though not all) stemmed from our manifestly pathetic attempts to run the office.

When Bryn Jones took over the UK chair, he worked furiously to promote Greenpeace to even greater heights. Bryn's style, however, didn't suit many of the staff, and conflicts soon arose. I spent much of my time in the office trying to build bridges, yet at every attempt was accused of betrayal by one side or the other. Simultaneously, the UK Board were accusing me of siding with McTaggart for wanting to bring in outsiders. I was in a cleft stick and things were coming to a head.

The straw that broke the camel's back was an issue on which Bryn and I, along with the rest of the board and staff, were completely united.

The UK is an important clearing house for the fur industry throughout the world. Every year, 40 million animals are killed to meet demand. A large percentage of them are caught with steel-jawed 'leg hold' traps which are outlawed in the very country which imports most of these pelts – the UK.

In 1984, Greenpeace UK had mounted a campaign designed to reduce the popularity of fur coats, by exposing the horror of these trapping methods. Within the space of a few months, the David Bailey billboards we had produced in the UK, depicting the lower half of a model trailing a fur coat from which issued a path of blood, were being displayed in South Africa, the United States and other countries all over the world.

An organisation called Indigenous Survival International, representing indigenous peoples who relied on fur-trapping for a living, fought back fiercely. It could be argued that the UK office had not done their homework as well as they should, and the plight of such communities did need greater consideration. But it was the commercial fur industry our campaign had sought to target, rather than isolated communities and genuine hunters.

Nonetheless, Greenpeace UK were instructed by Greenpeace International to abandon the campaign as indigenous peoples in the USA, Canada and Scandinavia were our traditional and historic allies. We were all outraged. The vast bulk of the animals were caught by weekend trappers killing for pin-money. Bryn, who had worked tirelessly on the campaign, saw it as perhaps the most vital attempt to fundamentally change public opinion towards the environment. He was determined to go down fighting.

In the newsletter he prepared in the spring of 1985, he apologised to the UK supporters and to the many celebrities and stars who had given their time to this popular campaign. In his editorial he castigated Greenpeace for their lack of courage, and vowed that the issue would be reinstated as soon as possible. That alone was enough to seal his fate. The cartoon he commissioned to accompany the editorial probably did the same for the entire UK board. Drawn by a renowned and respected cartoonist, Richard Willson, it depicted well-heeled trappers despatching a wolf held in a leg-hold trap, with a high-velocity rifle. The word 'inuit' had been bastardised across the jacket of the trapper to read 'nituit'.

It was a Sunday. I was about to leave for another campaign and was trying to smooth the waters between the UK board and McTaggart before I left. Bryn had drafted an apology for the cartoon and editorial to the outraged organisation, and I read it to McTaggart over the phone.

'Not enough, Peter,' he said. 'You'll have to tender your resignations – the whole board – to show the organisation you guys are prepared to relinquish control. You will probably be asked back to serve again once new members have been appointed, but you have to resign first.'

By offering to resign, I felt we had a slight chance of staying on the board. If we didn't resign, I thought we'd be out anyway. With great misgivings, the others were persuaded by me to do as was asked at the forthcoming board meeting.

It only lasted a few minutes. Bryn resigned from the Chair which was taken over by Sidney Holt, an internationally renowned whale expert whom we ourselves had invited to join the executive. Sidney moved the item of resignation of the existing board to the top of the agenda and we duly did what was expected. With that, he promptly adjourned the meeting and he and other new members vacated the room to a waiting taxi, leaving us behind. The blood drained from my face.

'What happened to our reinstatement Wilks?' asked Reg.

'The new board has declined to invite us back,' I spluttered.

'I'm sorry guys.'

The day held one more disaster for me. While I was drowning my considerable sorrows in matching quantities of beer, the new board members were ensconced in a hotel room with McTaggart, meeting my replacement, the new executive director – Alan Thornton. My depression was complete. I had been outmanouevred. I had swallowed McTaggart's hint that the board might invite us back and misled my colleagues. After years of unstinting work, at the point when the pain and anguish was about to show results, Thornton was there to enjoy it, not us. I left London the following day feeling as though I had had a leg amputated. Within a few weeks, the bulk of the staff at Greenpeace UK had resigned and Bryn had agreed to work with the new board to help the transition. A new era was beginning.

I left Graham Street and was seconded by the International Board to work with our Antarctic campaign team, working from the International headquarters in Lewes near the south coast of England. One long chapter had closed and another was opening.

During my time in Lewes, the International Whaling Commission was to hold its annual meeting in Bournemouth, also on England's south coast. McTaggart had asked two members of the Greenpeace International board (Monika Griefahn and myself) to meet him there in his hotel room to review the IWC Agenda.

It was 11am, July 10th, 1985. The town was basking in mid-summer sunshine. As we opened notebooks, the phone by McTaggart's bed rang three times before I answered it. It was a collect call from New Zealand from other members of the International board. I accepted the charge and handed the receiver to McTaggart, taking little notice of the conversation he had. In fact, he said very little. He hung up and looked at us.

His face was ashen and his words are seared in my memory: 'The Warrior's been sunk. There were two explosions. One guy's missing.'

I felt a cold, creeping horror. It had to be an accident. A failure in the engine room. It couldn't be sabotage. We weren't an extreme political organisation, we were a peaceful band of people fighting abuses of the environment. 'One guy's missing,' Mc Taggart had said. Agents of the French Secret Service had murdered our friend and colleague, Fernando Pereira. The cloak of innocence slipped from my shoulders, and I shivered.

The Rainbow Warrior had lain at harbour in Auckland, New Zealand, while being prepared for the Muroroa leg of her Pacific Odyssey. Shortly before midnight, a dull thud had shaken the ship, lifting crew members on board out of their seats. She immediately began to list and Davey Edward rushed to the engine room to see water pouring in through a hole in the hull. The shocked crew began to abandon ship on the skipper's orders, two crew being sent to search the lower cabins for sleeping occupants.

As the water rose to knee height, the temptation to recover personal equipment was strong. Fatally, Fernando decided to retrieve his expensive cameras and as he descended the stairs a second explosion rocked the ship. Crew now jumped to safety on the quayside and she began to

The Rainbow Warrior lies crippled at Marsden Wharf, Auckland, blown apart by two French limpet mines, July 1985. Fernando Pereira died on board *(Miller/Greenpeace)*.

sink fast, stern first. Fernando, caught by the rush of water, did not make it.

I drove my motorbike back to Lewes, screaming disbelief to the wind, kidding myself that tears which flowed copiously were caused by the speed and the cold. I couldn't come to terms with it. Even over the following few days when it was confirmed that two limpet mines had sunk the Warrior, I still believed there had been a monstrous mistake. I knew the facts, but refused to translate them into a rational conclusion. The sinking of the Warrior was my initiation into a world where governments kill when they run out of arguments.

The sinking of the Warrior and the death of Fernando catapulted the name Greenpeace into the farthest reaches of the globe. The frantic post-bombing activity caused us to change plans, divert ships and stretch our personnel to breaking point.

Those who had been attracted to Greenpeace by some vague ideological whim were suddenly thrust into an ugly reality. Even the most recent additions to the Greenpeace staff must have felt vulnerable in the weeks and months afterwards. I certainly did. It was clear that, having struck the raw nerve of French activities in the Pacific, Greenpeace would either have to change gear and capitalise on the wave of sympathy the bombing had generated, or shrink back from the effects of its own success. It collectively took a deep breath, bowed its head and, to everyone's eternal credit, marched forward.

Outright condemnation of the bombing was unequivocal. Only one country's voice was noticeably absent – that of the UK. The Warrior was a British-registered vessel and an act of terrorism had been perpetrated against what is technically a piece of UK territory. Mrs Thatcher, however, declined to criticise an ally.

The Warrior was sunk, but the protest at Muroroa had to go ahead despite her loss. The need to continue with it was greater than ever, in honour of the sunken ship. And for Fernando.

The decision to take Greenpeace into the fight over the future of Antarctica was visionary and controversial.

Typically, it was McTaggart who was at the centre of this vision: to establish the first, year-round, non-governmental scientific base on the continent at the bottom of the world.

Antarctica once formed part of an ancient super-continent called Gondwanaland. It was joined with Australia, New Zealand, Africa, India and South America and enjoyed a temperate or even semi-tropical climate. Continental drift forced the continents apart. Antarctica's existence, until the 17th century, was only guessed at. Contemporary explorers believed that a continent to the south was indeed there – if only to balance the land-masses in the northern hemisphere – and they dubbed it 'Terra Incognita', the unknown land.

Although early explorers confirmed the existence of a southern landmass, the area known as the Ross Dependency was only discovered 150 years ago. Scientific research dominated its history as soon as humankind found ways to survive the hostility of its winter storms, and it became the world's largest, most important and least contaminated laboratory. It still is.

In 1958 representatives of 12 nations agreed to meet regularly to discuss the future of the continent. The resulting Antarctic Treaty has been held up ever since as a shining example of how an international agreement should work. It calls for the Antarctic to be a demilitarised and non-nuclear zone, and attempts to freeze conflicts over territorial claims. However, the shine is not as bright as at first appears. Argentina, Chile and the UK all claim sections of land which overlap. Other claimants are France, Norway, Australia and New Zealand; but these claims are not recognised by most nations. The Treaty side-stepped the prickly issue of who 'owned' what. It merely postponed what could ultimately be a bitter, and perhaps bloody, dispute.

It has often been said that competing territorial claims and the existence of rich mineral deposits will cause armed conflict. In the opinion of some, this has already happened. For the British, the Falkland Islands provide a highly strategic 'home' port close to the Antarctic peninsula. To have that facility snatched from them, when the Argentinians invaded the Falklands in 1981, forced a battle which was just as much over convenient access to the potential mineral wealth of the Antarctic, as it was over the defence of British subjects.

The Antarctic Treaty makes no mention of minerals, or indeed of the living resources of the Antarctic – whales, seals, fish and krill. For this purpose, the Antarctic Treaty nations developed the Minerals Regime and the Living Resources Convention. Taking the latter first, it can be summed up as 'great thinking, shame about the implementation'. It has everything in it conservationists could ask for, but is largely ignored.

The Minerals Regime, on the other hand, had no redeeming features. Faced with what Treaty nations felt was the 'inevitability' of mining in the Antarctic, they sat down in the mid-80s to develop a strategy by which the mineral resources of Antarctica could be exploited without a gold-rush mentality. At least that was the public face of it. The negotiations were dominated, as usual, by the tactics of the big, powerful industrialised nations who had the resources to go in 'quick and dirty' (as conservationists called it).

If the expedition failed it would expose Greenpeace to the possible ridicule of the world. If it succeeded it would invade territory which the Antarctic Treaty Nations had for decades considered their sole preserve. It would also enable us to focus on the way some of the Treaty nations were ignoring their environmental responsibilities and – all importantly – if we set up a base, it would enhance our claim to observer status at the Antarctic Treaty meetings. From this position we could argue more directly for a ban on mineral mining.

The audacity of the idea appealed to me, yet it was no mean undertaking. Greenpeace had neither the means nor the experience to carry out such a plan with confidence. None of our ships was ice-class and no-one had more than brief experience of working a vessel in ice. Furthermore, it would commit a sizeable chunk of international funds to one campaign. Vociferous attacks came particularly from Greenpeace Germany, who argued with Teutonic logic that if we were opposed to human invasion of the Antarctic, why were we adding to that invasion by establishing our own base? It was only thanks to several more determined members of the organisation that the campaign became more than a lobbying exercise. The stakes were high indeed.

Greenpeace had recently been given an ex-ocean-going boat by the Maryland Pilots Association. Although she was offered to us gratis, she actually cost the organisation US$500,000 in 'finder's fees'. She was ill-equipped for ice work, and indeed to carry the mountain of equipment we would need, being a tug, not a cargo ship. McTaggart dismissed misgivings by pointing out that when we travelled the ice would be melting. Small yachts had made it to the Antarctic during the few short summer

Plate 1

The Classic Image: barrel of waste, ocean, Greenpeace. We oppose the dump of radioactive waste from the Gem, Atlantic, 1981 *(Gleizes/Greenpeace)*

Plate 2 Adelie Penguins strike up the dawn chorus, McMurdo Sound *(Schmidt/Swenson).*

Plate 3 Sunset over a tabular berg, Ross Sea, Antarctica *(Ken Ballard)*.

Plate 4

An icy wonderland. The m.v. Greenpeace viewed through an arched berg,
Cape Hallet, 1987 *(Ken Ballard)*.

Plate 5

Ten-tenths and still moving! The Gondwana was referred to as a floating bulldozer, and was purpose-built for ice work. Cape Hallett, 1989 *(Morgan/ Greenpeace)*.

Plate 6 Nice place, shame about the beach. Winterquarters Bay, McMurdo, is bordered by a rubbish tip of unimaginable proportions. US Coastguard vessel in background *(Sabine Schmidt)*.

Plate 7 Stop the bloody whaling! Greenpeace demonstrates its direct-action versatility by utilising its helicopter in the fight to save the whale *(Sabine Schmidt)*.

Plate 8 Orcas patrol the ice-edge in search of a meal. These family pods often number 30 plus *(Ken Ballard)*.

months, and we would in any case, have the ship's bow strengthened. The m.v. Greenpeace, as she was finally called (I wanted her to be named Antarctic Warrior) would replace the sabotaged Rainbow Warrior as our Pacific protest vessel, before sailing on her epic voyage.

But who would be our Antarctic campaigner? We sat around at an International board meeting scratching one name off the list after another. A stony silence followed the removal of the last name, and I doodled idly on my pad. Glancing up, I noticed the other four board members looking at me with decidedly silly grins on their faces.

'Oh NO, you guys. No way! No way! You're not getting ME on that ship going to the Antarctic. I like the weather WARM.'

I should have known McTaggart better.

Antarctica is stunning in its majesty and awesomeness. It should be saved for its beauty alone *(Ken Ballard)*.

10. Wilkinson's Erection

The prospect of going to Antarctica was at once exhilarating and simply out of the question. I was going through a period where there seemed a possibility of a reconciliation with my wife Annette, who had become estranged from me due to the ever-increasing pressure of work on my time. I was also concerned about the campaign profile of the UK office and its nuclear campaigns which were my first and abiding priority. Yet the Antarctic was somewhere I had always dreamt of. It was Scott, Amundsen, Ross, Shackleton and every childhood fantasy I had ever had all rolled into one.

I ached for the peace and quiet of my country cottage in Suffolk with its roses around the door and its honeysuckle arch, and I missed my wife, my dog and cats. But I knew that if I returned home, I would face the inevitability of my wanderlust, sooner or later.

Whilst I grudgingly accepted that I was the only logical choice, I also had a sneaking suspicion I was needed out of the way. Without me, the board would have an easier task of ramming through their changes in London. It was rumoured later that I had been banned to the Greenpeace equivalent of Siberia. Remi Parmentier, a colleague who steered the French office for years and who had printed on his business card 'Nasty Little Agitator', was likewise banished to the wilds of South America to establish Greenpeace there.

It wasn't until late in October 1985, when I was handed my ticket to Auckland, New Zealand, that I fully appreciated what I was about to do. The Antarctic! Across the remotest and wildest of seas! Following all my boyhood heroes! My stomach churned at the very thought of it.

I had been working in Lewes with Andy Hill, an ex-British Antarctic Survey smoothie recruited to put the expedition team together. Andy had in turn recruited Gerry Johnson, a tough uncompromising 24-year-old, also Antarctic experienced, to lead the team of four who would stay through the winter on Ross Island in the base we would construct for them on arrival. I had worked out a budget for the campaign and arrived at a figure a few dollars short of a cool million US. I submittted this to the board for comments prior to sending it to the Greenpeace Council, only to have McTaggart bursting into the office a day later screaming blue murder.

I had sent out a politically unacceptable budget. Although I felt it reflected a true estimate of the planning requirement, the sum actually

available – around $600,000, largely thanks to US and German film inter-
ests – left a shortfall of $400,000. As things moved on, the inevitable
happened, of course. The Council approved the amended budget, we over-
spent, and I got the blame.

I arrived in Auckland on a cold and wet night in late October and was
met at the airport by Carol Stewart and the late Elaine Shaw, two stalwarts of the New Zealand office. The first port of call was the quayside
where the refloated Rainbow Warrior lay dark and lifeless, gently tugging
at her mooring lines and creaking mournfully. I went on board. It was a
mistake.

The flashlight revealed upturned cabins, piles of crockery, broken hand-
basins, severed pipes and chaos. She was a ghost ship, and everywhere I
pointed the beam of the torch, I saw faces from happier times. I heard the
laughter, the throb of her engines and saw the pot-plants swaying as she
careered through one sea or another, rising to the swell, crashing into the
troughs. I went into the aft cabin which I had occupied so often, and I
peered into the tiny saloon, the venue for so many outrageous parties.
Empty, silent and grim, the Warrior stared through eyeless sockets at a
world she had done nothing to harm and so much to help. I turned the
torch off and stood in the dark, choking with sorrow.

The m.v. Greenpeace arrived two days later at the beginning of November. While I had been preparing to fly out to New Zealand, the crew
had been in Hamburg loading ton after ton of cargo into a ship which had
no cargo space to speak of. There had been much criticism of the 'land-
lubbers' in Greenpeace offices who had taken decisions which now required a crew to do a dangerous job with unsuitable tools.

Already enraged by the bombing of the Warrior and angered by the
unsuitability of this new vessel, the crew were also exhausted after a long
sea passage protesting at Muroroa against the very nation which had sunk
its flagship and killed a colleague. Despite the success of this protest,
they looked haggard and fraught. Seeing the Warrior and mooring alongside her did nothing for levity. Even greeting old friends was a muted
affair. Clearly their experiences over the past few months had left them
drained and bitter and within minutes of their arrival, many stood in small
groups on the quayside by the Warrior, grieving as I had.

So much was riding on the campaign that I was at pains to instil some
drive into everyone. They worked hard enough, and the new personnel,
particularly Gerry Johnson, helped enormously to drag the crew's minds
off the Warrior and onto the task ahead. But it was virtually impossible to
get the press interested. New Zealand had never experienced such notoriety before, and inevitably every press briefing about the Antarctic voyage
turned into one about the Warrior.

The weeks that followed were a portent of things to come. John Cas-

First mate Ken Ballard: the smile that broke a thousand hearts. Ken's motto: 'Never use mechanical means when brute force will do' *(Steve Morgan)*.

tle, the skipper, was in a particularly cussed mood. He was trying to come to terms with the Warrior's demise, the new and daunting Antarctic venture, the arrival of helicopter crews and other 'non-Greenpeace types', and the huge expenditure, all at once. Attempts at inspiring him failed. We had to look for a replacement skipper at short notice. Fortunately for us, Pete Bouquet, a veteran of early Warrior days, was available. He arrived in New Zealand with his family in tow, four kids and a wife.

Axel Engstfeld, a German film maker, had agreed to invest a considerable amount of money in the expedition on the agreement that he would make a film. He arrived with a soundman and cameraman to add to the confusion, as box after box of camera and lighting gear was hand-balled onto the ship to be squeezed somewhere below decks.

The ship was now a constant hive of activity. First mate Ken Ballard, strong, silent and sometimes professional to a painful degree, sat on the crane for hours, swinging gear on board and barking orders over a cacophony of disagreement as to where it should be stowed. The sections of the base itself, in which the overwintering scientists would live and carry out their projects, were arranged on the afterdeck, exposed to the elements and to the ravages of the Southern Ocean.

Gerry and the wintering team were busy checking off list after list of equipment, counting packets of soup and poring over survival gear. A stream of vehicles disgorged a never-ending supply of food for the ship and the base. The skipper and mates scrutinised the charts and ice maps, making incomprehensible calculations as to the ship's trim and stability, given the load she was required to carry and conditions we were likely to meet. And all the time, the Warrior bore silent witness to this unfair attention to her successor, and acted as a magnet for some of the crew who felt she needed their attention more than the expedition.

Then Andy Hill, our logistics co-ordinator and overseer of the construction team, dropped a bombshell. Due to illness in the family he wasn't able to go to the Antarctic with us either. We scoured the world by phone seeking a replacement with suitable Antarctic experience. With five days to go, Doug Allen, a former colleague of Gerry's, agreed to drop his life and come with us.

The subject of our expedition had been discussed at a closed session of the Antarctic Treaty Consultative Parties, the self-appointed arbiters of Antarctica's future. They were outraged at our effrontery, particularly that we were planning to build a base, and the Australian and New Zealand delegates had been urged by their colleagues to 'do something about it.'

Australia's instructions to do something made themselves apparent in the form of their Science Minister, Barry Jones. He visited the ship and brought with him the press, and a Scotsman who had allegedly helped build the m.v. Greenpeace. In front of cameras and assembled journalists, Jones implied that our amateurism was a threat to our lives, and also to the 'legitimate' bases in the Antarctic whose personnel would have to risk their own lives to rescue us when we foundered. He publicly begged us not to go.

When that failed, he rounded on the new skipper, Pete Bouquet, and demanded to know the hull thickness. Pete, clearly nervous at the onslaught, said he thought it was 20mm plating.

'Nine! Nine only!!' piped up the Scotsman. 'This is not a polar vessel. You'll put yourselves in awful peril if you go down south.'

The newspapers lapped it up. We did our best to boost each other's flagging confidence; nonetheless it began to eat away at Pete's faith in the ship. More to the point it was getting to Pete's wife, Jane, who was to stay in New Zealand when we sailed. I revelled in the cut and thrust of campaigning banter, even offering the Science Minister a deal whereby if Australia declared the Antarctic a World Park, I would call off the expedition. But the fact was that he had done his job admirably well, and we all privately began to doubt our capacity to complete the task.

The day before we left, a piece of cargo arrived which had the crew in a state of mutiny. In the planning stages of the expedition, it had been agreed that a visible commemoration marking the voyage would be brought with us for erecting at Ross Island. McTaggart was a keen advocate of this idea and employed a team of designers in the States to draw up plans for it. I had contacted Nobel Peace Prize winner Johan Galtung, to write some suitably noble words for the monument, and promptly forgot about it until the truck arrived at the quayside with two enormous boxes. There was no deck space left to stow it, and Pete was already worrying about the stability of the ship.

After placating the crew as best I could, we agreed to remove the packaging to reduce its bulk and put the thing together to see the nature of the beast. Bolts had to be hammered through stainless steel legs and the wharf reverberated to the deafening sound of metal on metal for three hours until the 6-metre high structure could be appreciated in all its awkward, garish and totally unsuitable detail. The noise did not endear the crew to this monstrosity which was, after all, supposed to be a tribute to the qualities of the Antarctic, one of which is its silence. It was unsportingly called Wilkinson's Erection. As it came aboard to be stowed in front of the main mast, Wolf the crane driver, dangled it from a hook over the water. He turned to the sweating crew on the quayside.

'Well? Shall I?'

The jeers and hoots of approval rang in my ears as I made my way up the gangplank. I was afraid about this trip; the crew were not enthusiastic and the skipper had to take an awkwardly stowed and unsuitable ship through terrible conditions. We faced two months at sea. We could only pray for good weather.

11. Bottom of the World

We were finally ready to embark upon our great adventure south. I studied the charts on the bridge. After two days sailing from Melbourne we would be clear of the inhibiting influence of land masses. It is here, in the Roaring Forties, that the seas can build up to monstrous heights. Into the Furious Fifties and then the Screaming Sixties we would go to enter the Ross Sea – provided we could negotiate the outer ice pack successfully. The prospect was daunting, yet I was fired with excitement. The world's eyes were on us and our fortunes, the future of Greenpeace lay in our hands, and I was going to see Terra Incognita, the Last Continent. At that point I could have hugged McTaggart for giving me this once-in-a-lifetime opportunity. And it was time to go!

The routine at sea on a working ship is odd. The vessel is most times almost deserted as different watches take their rest, or the effects of seasickness force people involuntarily to their bunks as the swell of the open ocean treats the craft like a plaything. For the campaigner on board, it's imperative to fight sea-sickness as quickly as possible. You have to be available for crew meetings, for press calls and for watches. I suffered badly every time I sailed. No remedy ever worked for me successfully. I threw up where I was, returning to what I was doing as best I could. Your bunk becomes a refuge of sleep, warmth and comfort, a womb into which you eagerly crawl to blot out the awfulness. The call for watch duties comes like a death sentence. Dreams are vivid and stay with you for hours. The sea entrances you, beats you, and eventually becomes part of you.

The mantle of doubts and anxiety slipped from the ship the further we drew away from land. Soon we were into the familiar round of watches, meals and deck duties. Christmas was organised to be enjoyed as traditionally as possible.

The burden of responsibility for all our lives was shouldered by Pete Bouquet, a highly experienced veteran. He had been asked to step in at the last moment to skipper an unsuitable ship and a largely inexperienced crew through the world's most treacherous seas to the most inhospitable place on earth. My relationship with him would be critical to the success of the voyage. Ideally, skipper and campaigner should form a team: any rift in this relationship rapidly transmits itself to the rest of the ship. But I couldn't get close to Pete; he shouldered his burden alone.

As we neared the ice, Pete became more preoccupied. No more than a handful of ships venture into these hazardous waters each year. Lookouts were doubled.

Axel Engstfeld was busy around the ship directing his film team. He interviewed Pete several times and his theme was, naturally, how Pete felt about the trip given the limitations of the ship, the inexperience of most of the crew and the high stakes riding on the expedition. I later saw these interviews which were shot in classic Gothic-style with severe shadows falling across Pete's face as he smiled, admitted his fears and shrugged. The interview with Gerry Johnson, on the other hand, was full of joy as he contemplated a year in his beloved Antarctica.

Cliques began to develop on board. While this is a natural consequence of forcing 30 people to live cheek by jowl for months on end, I noticed that those with Antarctic experience had formed an unofficial advisory board and were offering muttered warnings as to the advisability of certain courses of action. The film crew were naturally a tight unit, and Gerry, Ken Ballard and I gravitated together on watch and in the saloon during 'r and r' time.

Snowfall on the ship gave us a chance to loosen up. Ken, Gerry and I were beside ourselves with delight as we rushed from one bridge wing to the next pelting each other with snowballs. Pete stormed onto the bridge.

'You're supposed to be watch-keeping, not prancing about like a bunch of schoolboys!' he spat.

He was utterly justified and Gerry apologised on behalf of the watch, but my relationship with him deteriorated from there.

We cautiously pushed further and further south. Our first iceberg had everyone lining the rails and we could see the outer ice pack many miles away on the horizon. In the wake of the berg, a litter of bergy-bits and growlers trailed in a swell deadened by the weight of the millions of tons of ice ahead.

As the ship nosed her way into thicker stuff, Pete went to the crow's nest atop the mainmast to look for leads into the ice sheet we would have to penetrate. The film crew were making the most of a glorious day and our first experience of serious Antarctic ice fields. We lowered an inflatable, and shot film from the dinghy as the ship nudged a lump of ice. It gave the impression of ice-breaking, and we fired the photos off to the news agencies hoping it would run. I hoped fervently the Australian press would pick it up. I wanted the Science Minister to choke on his morning cornflakes.

At 1900 every evening, we had a radio schedule with the vessel Southern Quest which was on her way south to collect three adventurers from Ross Island led by Robert Swan, who were walking all the way to the pole 'in the footsteps of Scott'. Southern Quest was further south than us, deep in the ice, being classified as Ice-Class 1 with a reinforced bow and keel.

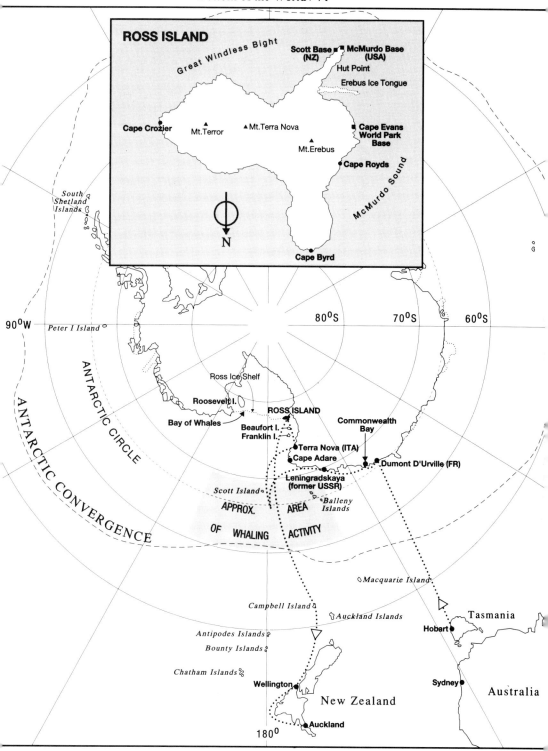

Antarctica, illustrating its geographical relationship to New Zealand and Australia, the bases visited by Greenpeace, and the route of the m.v. Gondwana between December 1988 and February 1989. Inset: Ross Island.

Her skipper cajoled us every evening; 'Come on in, the ice is great!' He insisted that there were many leads and they were making progress. Pete resisted the temptation, thankfully.

We spent several days trailing carefully along the ice edge, still sailing south, when suddenly we were in open water. The Ross Sea opened to welcome us with placid waters and spectacular ice-bergs.

After a few days, the Southern Quest failed to come up for their 'sked'. We didn't think much of it, as operational difficulties can often interfere with reception or transmission. However, after the second night of no contact we called the American base on McMurdo Sound to ask if they had news of her. They told us starkly 'The Southern Quest sank 36 hours ago. All personnel are safe.' She had been squashed by the ice like a piece of plywood, and sank within minutes.

The news stunned us all. The effect on Pete was shattering. He declared 'Well, that's it. We take a look and if the ice is too bad, we get out of this awful place.'

The Quest's shipwrecked crew had been in no immediate danger, and had planned their route to the safety of the shores of Ross Island and their small hut, across a series of large ice-floes. But US helicopters had arrived and begun ferrying them to McMurdo where they were immediately put aboard one of the giant C130 transport planes and whisked back to New Zealand. The Americans had a strict policy of non-cooperation with non-governmental expeditions. The crew had no option but to comply, and found themselves unable to use their own resources to extricate themselves, so swift was the US response. They also had to abandon their equipment, including a small aeroplane. Later the Footsteps organisers received a hefty bill from the Americans.

A three day run to the inner ice-pack would determine how we could operate over the coming weeks. Little or no ice would let us enter McMurdo Sound only a few miles from Cape Evans where we intended to establish the wintering base on Ross Island. Heavy ice would force us to wait until it broke up as the summer wore on. But few were interested in the policies of waiting. Axel had the daily costs of keeping a film crew on board, the overwinterers were anxious to start their projects, and Edwin Mickleburgh, a photographer and writer, needed us to get on with setting up the base for the purposes of his book.

As we approached a point 100 miles from Ross Island the ice was thicker than ever. Pete went up in the helicopter for a recce. Even from the ship we could see a sheet of fast ice stretching in an uninterrupted sheen way to the south – our route to the base site we had chosen. Gerry, Ken and I sat disconsolately in the saloon with a group of others awaiting his return. We heard the clatter of the tiny chopper as it landed on sheets of plywood roped atop the cargo on the aft deck to serve as our 'helipad'.

A few moments later, Pete walked into the saloon pulling off his gloves.

'There's no way through.' he said. 'In the interests of safety, I'm turning the ship round and heading north.'

He was gone, and a few minutes later the sun marched across the bulkhead as the ship swung through 180 degrees. My heart lurched.

Gerry held his head in his hands. 'What's the point of coming all this way, only to go home when we see what we knew would be there anyway?'

'We're not going home, Gerry,' I said, 'We're getting out of the way of the pack ice.'

'Then how come we're steaming at ten knots? He never wanted to come in the first place. He's taking a look and getting out.'

I slumped in my chair. I knew Pete was in an untenable position. The Southern Quest was far stronger than our vessel, yet she had been crushed easily. The danger was obvious to us all, yet everyone also knew the importance of the voyage to the future of Greenpeace. This is where my allegiance lay. I could not give up easily. We had spent two weeks plugging through the Southern Ocean, dodging ice and icebergs to get close to our goal, and a few hours after arriving we were turning about to steam back.

Ken and Gerry looked at me in desperate appeal.

'It's early summer.' Ken said. 'The ice can only get better. It's you Wilks, you're the campaigner.'

I went to Pete's cabin and knocked. He was a man shouldering a huge burden. We cracked a couple of beer cans and looked each other in the eye.

12. Nightmare Voyage

Pete was in no mood to risk the ship and the lives of the crew in this part of the Ross Sea, for what he now considered a foolhardy venture, and I knew enough not to question his decision. We tip-toed round the issues for an hour, but he was going north and that was that. He did finally agree to slow down so that we could assess our situation and explore the idea of alternative landfalls.

After watch, as was customary, the 8-12 watch had a few drinks, and then our joint despair at heading away from Ross Island magicked a bottle of rum from someone's cabin. Around 3am, John Welsh and I staggered off to our berth very much worse for wear. My fitful slumber was interrupted by John stomping out of the cabin. 'You want some aspirins, Wilks?' he offered. He was gone an inordinate length of time and I went looking for him. He was in the galley propped up by the microwave oven melting ice-cubes to make enough liquid to wash down the aspirins. Pieter, the chief engineer, had turned off the water without telling anyone, to ration our supplies. We lurched back to the cabin, cursing Pieter loudly and giggling to ourselves.

It was now the middle of January. Our days were spent heading north at four knots away from our destination, whale watching, and spotting familiar icebergs. The crew were restless, and to give them some sort of yardstick I agreed with Pete that we should establish a cut-off date when we would abandon the attempt to find an alternative landfall and head back to New Zealand. The time we had left to establish the base was waning with every day, but I still held out hope that if we couldn't build the base before the short summer was over, we could at least off-load fuel, the sections of the base itself, and other equipment, in readiness for next year. The idea wasn't popular, least of all with the film crew who were seeing the chances of getting decent footage fading fast and didn't want to incur more costs than were necessary. I often found Axel huddled in a corner with members of the ship's crew, endlessly discussing how, when and why we should be heading north. It was an endless topic all over the ship.

We slowed down further. I wanted to go south again, Pete wanted to get home. Fog closed in and we could see nothing, so we stopped altogether. The atmosphere on board deteriorated. My diaries record that we were 'fogbound, stationary, with tempers flaring . . . ship's fuel begun to wax . . . complaints about food on board and petty arguments surface with increasing regularity . . . Gerry ready to throw in the towel on "shambolic Greenpeace". . . Pete in perpetual black mood . . .' We seemed to be constantly surrounded by whales, mostly minkes and orcas, and only this took the edge off the atmosphere.

Three days after we started to sail north – three days of friction and rising tensions – Pete's mood brightened. He became almost light-hearted, and announced changes to the watches to remove some of the tensions. After a meeting between him, the mates, some of the crew, Ken, Gerry and myself, he finally agreed to turn about and sail south once again. I was relieved, but at the same time concerned at the depths of his mood swings. Then he suggested a plan.

The Footsteps of Scott expedition, which had earlier lost the Southern Quest, had a ready-made base at Cape Evans where their polar walkers had spent the previous winter. Our original strategy had been to build as close as possible to the American base at McMurdo Sound which was being polluted shamelessly. The base was approximately 15 miles from McMurdo and it was not entirely suitable being rather small for our needs, but it could be useful, if we were unable to establish our own base and if we could get permission to use it. Pete now suggested that we return to the coast, staying out of the ice, and that we use the helicopter to check it out. If we couldn't go in, then we'd head straight home.

I wanted to stay in the area as long as was sensibly safe to achieve as many of our objectives as possible. The ice was certainly thicker than expected, but it was bound to clear as the month wore on. To bolster my opinion, I sent a telex to Roger Wilson (my immediate boss in Lewes) asking that he instruct us to stay a further four weeks. I needed some support from beyond the confines of the ship.

The next day we held a crew meeting to discuss Pete's plan and other alternatives. It was a very fractured and aggressive affair. Above the noise of the engines and the scrape of ice against the hull, people shouted their opinions with frightening invective. Edwin Mickleburgh stormed out of the saloon, demanding that we abandon the venture forthwith and return to Auckland.

But at last, after days of uncertainty, we managed to reach accord. We would continue heading south, and we would not turn home again until it was clear that our task was hopelessly beyond us. In short, we had a common purpose, and this at last seemed to lighten the crew. As I wearily made my way to the communications shack during the evening to send another update to Roger, I noticed a telex in the machine ready for sending. It had been prepared by Edwin, and was an appeal to McTaggart to instruct me to abandon the expedition. In it, Edwin accused me of holding those on the ship hostage.

I read the telex with rising anger. I ripped it from the machine and stalked off in search of Edwin. I was furious: we had begun to unite the crew at last. His action would torpedo these hard-won seeds of harmony and I wanted his blood. I found him in the saloon and demanded his presence in the radio shack.

I read out sections of his telex: '. . . the winterers agree with my contention that Wilkinson is holding the ship and the crew to ransom . . .'

'Is that true, Edwin?' I asked.

'Well, that's certainly the impression I have,' he replied, flushing a little.

'Then let's go and ask them, shall we? Something you should have done before committing such an opinion to a telex.'

'But it's midnight. Leave it until the morning,' he suggested.

'Now, Edwin. We'll do it NOW.'

Putting the winterers on the spot like this was difficult, but I had to establish whether these four people wanted to abandon the voyage – they had prepared for their year in Antarctica, physically and psychologically, over a long period of time. They each gave a candid opinion, and though resigned to probably not setting up our own base, they were divided as to whether or not we should still keep trying for land.

I turned to Edwin and attempted to regain some of my flagging authority:

'Your presence on this ship is for the purposes of recording and documenting. If you even think about sending that telex, I'll take your notebook and ram it up your arse. Your book may well follow. Goodnight'

We had calm on board until Pete Bouquet roused me at 4am in a fury. Roger's telex had arrived in response to mine, agreeing to my cut-off date, the 20th of February. I myself had sown further discontent. Pete had had a much earlier date in mind.

Our renewed misery was enhanced when the Footsteps of Scott Expedition refused us permission to use their hut. The UK Foreign Office had told them not to cooperate.

Arriving once again within sight of Ross Island we found that, despite the lateness of the season, we couldn't get much closer than last time. There were great carpets of floating pack ice which should by now have melted. We were many miles away round the Cape by ship, but as the crow flies, we were only 30 miles from our goal. It was a terrible time. If we went home we'd fail our supporters. If we went in we risked everything, including our lives.

We stooged around in grey weather, bucking force 8 gales, trying to decide what to do and watching the ice, time running out. It was approaching the fag-end of January. We were informed by McMurdo base, just by way of additional pressure, that they would shortly cease operating their

The m.v. Gondwana ploughs through ice off the Balleny Islands. This ice-strengthened vessel bought specifically for polar work, was an ideal tool in later expeditions *(Greenpeace)*.

supply ships, ice cutters and coastguard vessels.

The inference was, 'there will be no help available for you guys if you get into trouble, so get out now.' To add to our woes, an approaching US ice-breaker reported 14 miles of ice pack now to the north of us. This put Pete in an understandable panic. On board, some were close to breaking point. Bernt, the giant German cameraman, threatened to 'tell the world' he was held 'hostage'. He and Axel began chanting 'no more waiting'. Taking the bull by the horns I ordered the helicopter up again.

Clear water was to be found to the north, though large slabs of ice ominously languished to the west. These could at any time push back towards the coast, crushing any unsuspecting, non-ice-class vessel in their path.

It was too risky to take the ship further in, but the existence of ice-free water lifted my hopes considerably. We needed six to eight weeks construction time to build the base, and that was clearly out of the question now, but there was still a faint hope that we might get to Ross Island to carry out environmental assessments and off-load the fuel and base camp sections ready for next year's attempt.

Calculating that two weeks would be sufficient for this, I agreed a new cut-off date with Pete. It would be the 5th February, not the 20th. I hoped this would meet everyone's needs. For the next few days, life was comparatively normal and pleasant. Pete calmed down and accepted his fate.

The helicopter was used daily, ferrying people back and forth to look at Ross Island, taking film crew and photographers over the intended site of the base camp and over McMurdo Station. After the day's operations, Pete would take us away from the shifting seas of ice which still refused to disperse.

During this continually fractious time we declared 'World Park Antarctica Day' to provide ourselves with a focus and, hopefully, a much-needed news story. We resolved to celebrate it at the Bay of Whales which was ice free, some 36 hours steaming to the east. Here the crew could set foot on the Ross Ice Shelf, not quite the Lost Continent, but good enough. The Shelf is a huge, floating swathe of ice which stretches 400 miles from east to west. Amundsen built his base camp at the Bay of Whales, a natural indentation in the Shelf, before his victorious race to the pole, beating Scott by a month.

We arrived on the 28th January 1986. Pete nudged the bow of the m.v. Greenpeace against the ice. It was no more than a metre deep at the water's edge, but rose gently to the slopes of the interior beyond a series of ice-falls, which guarded a plateau beyond. We were at the seaward extremity of this quite staggering Antarctic phenomenon, originally named by Ross who arrived there in 1840 when whales had been present in sufficient numbers for him to have no alternative but to call it after these amazing creatures.

Gerry and other more athletic crew members shimmied over the bow of the ship to dig holes in the ice into which hot water was poured once the 'deadmen' had been dropped in. These were heavy lumps of timber to which the ship's warps were attached. The hot water froze quickly, ensuring a firm hold for the vessel after she had gone broadside to the ice.

Leopard seals, crab-eater seals, Emperor and Adelie penguins dotted the ice and seemed oblivious to our arrival. I wrote in my diary: 'Refrain from going ashore until I can go with people manifesting respect for this place. My personal feeling of intrusion grows. It is beautiful.'

I finally went ashore when most of the crew were exploring the further reaches of the ice shelf. I spent two hours sketching the obliging penguins who ignored me and the biting wind, curling up their toes away from the ice and resting on their heels.

Despite all the briefings about the dangers, some of the crew cavorted under ice-falls, potentially lethal places. Soon, Pete was required to sound the recall claxon and terminate further gaiety. A second shift of people continued the party during the night, and I was woken at 0200 by singing and dancing, shouting and general yahooing. Looking out of my porthole,

I saw people dancing naked in the midnight sun.

We left the exquisite Bay of Whales at noon the following day. I felt sure it would not mourn our departure. We took the necessary pictures which we would use to demonstrate the way we celebrated 'World Park Day': not of naked cavorting but of the crew arranged down the gang-plank of the ship holding banners which had been cobbled together during the previous few days. It was adequate under the circumstances, but it was a stage-managed togetherness.

As we put the final touches to our call for a World Park, and demanded No-mining Status for Antarctica, we still didn't know whether we would now be able to make one last-ditch attempt to land at Ross island, or whether we would have to sail north and home.

We were tired. Most on board felt we had done enough. However, news reached the ship that the ice in McMurdo Sound was breaking up at last. We headed in, only to be confronted yet again, with vast, white, impenetrable expanses.

That night everything exploded. Chief engineer Davey Edward was so wound up that he pitched into two of his fellow engineers, accusing them of laziness. As I hustled him away he broke down sobbing with genuine sorrow. There followed an endless round of carping and criticising. Then Warren the helicopter mechanic 'resigned', saying he'd had it playing batman to a pilot pretending he was flying bi-planes in the Great War. Despite the brief levity his short-lived rebellion brought, the truth was that many of us were at breaking point.

Pete, the skipper, came into his own. He told us the crew would henceforth run the ship and have no part in decision making: non-crew such as Edwin, Doug and the film crew would be required to act in a manner fitting their role – as passengers. As for me, he foresaw no further need for me to act in any other capacity than that of a crew member as, in his fateful words,

'I'm altering course again. We're going home.'

It was perhaps my failure to cement a working partnership with Pete, more than anything else, which had caused the factions, the tensions, the disagreements. He was clearly sagging under an intolerable burden of responsibility, and (had I but known it) he had heard that his wife was being harassed by an unwelcome admirer back in Auckland. Before the voyage was out, he was treating me with open contempt. We spoke no more than the perfunctory necessities for the rest of the journey, and it was to be three years before our relationship got back on an even keel after this terrible voyage.

The mood on board in the days that followed was captured in my diary entries for the 2nd February: 'Course due north, following sea, heavy roll. Bored, worried, and sick of it all.' We had tried – and failed – to break new ground for Greenpeace. We'd spent a fortune, diverted money from other campaigns and badly let down our supporters.

Bernt, the giant German cameraman, suddenly livened up at the prospect of getting home. From the depths of his parka jacket pocket, he produced a scarce and very precious table-tennis ball.

The engineers set to work below decks making a net, table and bats faced both sides with rubber. Bernt continually warned people about the delicate nature of his ping-pong ball and we all treated it with loving care, as we lumped our way out of the Antarctic towards more temperate climes.

It was difficult to gauge the flight of the ball. When it was mid-air after bouncing off the table, the ship would pitch or roll. The ball would continue its descent while the environment in which it fell moved to the side or dropped ten feet. It made good entertainment and served to lighten the atmosphere. The first championship ended and we were about to begin another round when the keeper of the holy ball, Bernt himself, stepped backwards and squashed it flat.

Wellington was to be our first New Zealand port of call. We had been warned by radio that various political dignitaries were awaiting us, together with the usual press coterie. The crew stood on deck watching the approach of the quay in a mesmerised stupor. The invasion of our strange little world was at hand. Strangers were soon to swarm all over the ship, their presence an intrusion into our grief and disappointment. All at once, this crew which had been so disparate and so fractured, came together in a closing of ranks which generated its own warmth and closeness. People began to cry, others to hug each other.

Those last few hundred metres of water to the quayside in Wellington were the most painful I had ever crossed. I could not hide in my cabin and wish the time away. As we moored, microphones were thrust at me across the guard rail and before I knew what was happening, I was on automatic, trotting out the clichés and the denials of failure.

The stay in Wellington was brief. Two days later the ship slipped her moorings and nosed her way towards her home port of Auckland. On board were some strangers, hangers on, friends of friends and wives, boyfriends and lovers. One was Fiona Weightman, a tall, blonde Greenpeace volunteer who had been offered a trip on the ship by way of thank-you for all the work she had dedicated to Greenpeace. Those men who had been female-starved on board the ship eyed her hungrily and that night after watch, we were all to be found on the monkey-island on top of the bridge, supping beer, listening to music and gazing at a million stars set in an inky black panoply, and at Fiona. I moved just a fraction faster than anyone else. We formed a relationship that was to last three years.

The voyage was over. The ship near-empty. Ken Ballard, my cabin-mate John Welsh and I prepared to leave the ship and fly home to England. It was a blisteringly hot day in late February when we dragged our bags from the ship and dumped them on the sticky tarmac of the quayside. Two Americans sauntered up and shook hands. They had just flown in from the US base at McMurdo. The larger of the two adjusted his sunglasses and said, 'You guys did well to focus so much attention on the Antarctic. But there's a question I've been busting to ask. Why in hell did you leave so early? Christ, it's still high summer down there. A few days after you left, McMurdo was ice-free.'

We looked at each other. I mumbled an apology and slid into a waiting cab. Ken and John got in beside me and the cab drew away, leaving our American friends standing there in the sunlight. We said nothing to each other. I could not help the stream of tears which coursed down my cheeks into my beard and dripped gently onto my shirt. I silently vowed I would be back.

13. Doing it Properly

Arriving in London in April 1986, I went to see McTaggart. 'If another trip's on this coming year, I'll go again as the campaigner,' I told him. 'I'm not going to bow out of Greenpeace on that sort of note.'

I was back in New Zealand within six weeks, refreshed and rested. This time, I was in control from the very beginning rather than dragged in at the last minute.

We hired a warehouse in Auckland and began ferrying over sections of the base camp which had remained boxed and uninspected for 18 months. Some sections had warped, and we quickly dispensed with the outer shell – provided as a wind-break – saving ourselves three tons at a stroke. We were determined that the campaign to have Antarctica declared a World Park would have a physical outpost on the continent we were trying to protect. This time we would make it.

All the scientific and esoteric arguments about Antarctica's importance as a laboratory, its critical impact on global weather patterns and its function as a refuge for wildlife, pale into insignificance when one is faced with the sheer, staggering majesty of the place. Antarctica should be preserved for its beauty alone.

As the m.v. Greenpeace made its laborious way through the Southern ocean towards the great white continent for the second time, thoughts of the previous year were uppermost in my mind. We had had the misfortune to meet the worst ice conditions in twenty years. This year we had taken every precaution against a repeat of the tensions and animosities, yet there was still no guarantee we would get through – and we were going back in the same ship. We had no other. Even if we did get through, there was no promise we would have sufficient time to construct the base if the weather was against us. The potential was there for all the old frustrations to surface again. Wary though I was, we had left in high spirits.

Time and time again, I had dinned it into the heads of the crew that we would not be making decisions by voting or by any other method than that of autocracy. As the skipper was in charge of the ship, as the chief engineer was in charge of the engine room and as the pilot was in charge of the helicopters, so I was in charge of the campaign. It was the decision-making process more than anything else on the previous trip which had wrought confusion and dissent.

I need not have worried. We had the cream of Greenpeace activists on board. This was the most expensive and imaginative voyage Greenpeace had ever undertaken, and the crew were united in their determination to make it work.

The core of the expedition team – the gang of five as they became known (Ken Ballard, Martini Gotje, Henk Haazen, Jim Cottier and myself) – had been responsible for making most of the appointments and Marine Division, 12,000 miles away, had only imposed a few crew members without consultation. However, even these 'newcomers' were quickly assimilated into shipboard life and infected by the atmosphere of purpose and determination.

Jim Cottier was skipper, and nowhere could you have found a more genial and understanding captain. Jim exudes authority in the most benign manner. Despite all its vulnerability, he loved the ship and had confidence in it. He would not brook reminders that we might not get through.

'Course we'll get through!' he'd chastise me with a toss of his head.

Ken Ballard, veteran of ten years on Greenpeace ships, was again first mate. He was the backbone of the ship and my mentor on the 8-12 watch. We had sailed on the Cedarlea together, and on the Rainbow Warrior. Ken's motto is 'Never do something with a machine when you can whack it with a lump of wood'. Most of the time it worked.

With me on the 8-12 watch under Ken, were Jon Welsh and Chris Robinson. We trudged to the bridge just before 8 every morning, left it just after noon, then trudged back again at 8 in the evening to be relieved at midnight. So it went, day after day, seemingly forever as the ship rolled and pitched her way south, away from the warmth of New Zealand and into the cold and permanent daylight of the Antarctic summer. We crept across the chart at a pace slightly faster than one can run, making the 2,000 mile voyage in eleven days. I pitied those who flew. To experience the Antarctic in its full glory, one should earn this reward by facing the rigours of the ocean crossing: a tiny speck of metal being tossed on the great grey-bearded rollers of the southern ocean.

I often asked myself why the hell I was there as I clung to the wind-torn guard rail, watching the last of my dinner hit the boiling surf. But there was a purposeful and infectious buzz around the ship as we crept towards the mid-Sixties and into the iceberg belt. We set up a sweepstake. The winner had to correctly guess the attitude in which the first berg would be spotted. The prize was a helicopter ride of their choice later in the trip.

The weather worsened. Albatrosses glided effortlessly around the ship, mocking our cumbersome progress. And there were whales – 'Whales! There, and there, and another pod over here! – give me the binoculars, tell the guys in the mess quickly "Whales off the port bow!" '

Then there it was, looming out of the grey.

A huge, flat-topped battleship of ice, impervious to the wind and the 30-foot waves and the driving snow. Serene and majestic proof we were nearing Antarctica.

To those who have never before cast eyes on an iceberg, the experience often leaves them breathless, speechless or, in a few cases, tearful. The newer bergs, those only recently 'calved' from the ice shelf and freed from their terrestrial chains, are angular and sheer-sided. Older ones which have suffered for years the ravages of wind and sea erosion are unpredictable in shape. They can be rounded, becaved, lop-sided, turreted or a combination of all. Eventually, a berg becomes unstable. The section under water diminishes to the bulk of the section above and spectacular capsizes follow. Before a capsize though, a berg can live the life of a permanently drunken sailor, rolling from side to side at the mercy of the seas. They may take decades to melt completely as they reach warmer waters, or they may become 'growlers', iron-hard lumps of ice which can vary in size from that of a wardrobe to something as big as a small house. These float all but submerged. They are the hardest to spot, and are capable of holing a ship easily.

Forgotten were the days of inescapable nausea, the months of back-breaking preparation, the rows, the telexes. The sight of that chunk of ice, some three kilometres long, weighing a few million tons, was enough to make coming through Hell itself worthwhile.

We spent several hours circling the monster, cameras click-clicking

The m.v. Greenpeace, steams into McMurdo Sound, the Barne Glacier forming a spectacular backdrop *(Loor/Greenpeace)*.

every few seconds, until we were sated. It was hard to believe that within a few days we would be so blasé that even the most enthusiastic reports of 'you've-never-seen-one-like-this' would raise only the hardiest of bergophiles from their bolt-holes round the ship.

Into the Ross Sea sailed the good ship Greenpeace. Calmer waters now, afforded by the shelter of the coast off to the west; the Sixties gave way to the Seventies. Only eight degrees to go – a mere 480 miles, just over two days, steaming. Jim Cottier paced the bridge as we deckies, flushed with the responsibility of steering the ship through the bands of ice strewn across our path, hauled on the wheel to point the bow into clear water. Once or twice the ship had nowhere to go and Jim would crank the telegraph to 'Stop'. There followed an anxious few moments before the engineers could respond to the command and all eyes would be riveted to the rev counter, willing it to register zero. Then the engine noise would die and the ship would glide in silence towards wall-to-wall ice. All were conscious that only nine millimetres of steel protected the warmth and comfort of the ship's interior from the icy inhospitality of the Antarctic waters. The 'CRUNCH!' was immediately followed by a sideways lurch which would have the cooks cursing in the galley, and those sleeping irreverently jolted awake.

Progress was slow but spectacular as we weaved our way closer and closer to Ross Island. Adelie penguins stared at us from ice-floes with a look of constant incredulity on their faces. Snoring seals would wake with alarm and snort disapproval at having their icy raft rocked by the ship's wake. Whales would hold their course as they swam with mysterious purpose across our bows, diving at the last second beneath the hull. And ever-present was the picture-postcard backdrop of the Trans-Antarctic Mountains off to the west, purple, black and turquoise amid the myriad hues of blue, rising loftily and serenely to a series of peaks. What a place! What a beautiful, breath-taking place! It had been like this for millennia, and so few had seen it.

Next in the procession of sights in store for us was the Ross Ice Shelf, that awesome wall 70-100 feet high, which regularly calves massive chunks of floating ice. The largest ever recorded was estimated to be the size of Belgium – one berg, called B9 and a mere 22 by 90 kilometres was to calve the year following this voyage, taking the Bay of Whales with it.

Now it was time to make a bid for land. We waited a week, sending the helicopter up daily to reconnoitre the patterns of ice and to espy free water through it. Eventually, Jim came to me beaming his usual, uplifting and enthusiastic grin.

'Well, Wilks, there's a route through and we'll only have to nose a few floes out of the way. Let's have a go at it, shall we?'

Crew crowded the rails as we pushed forward into the pack at a snail's

Don't look now: the vulnerable m.v. Greenpeace surrounded by ice-floes weighing 'a few thousand tons'. Clear water was reached after a 12-hour struggle and a partial evacuation of the ship *(Loor/ Greenpeace).*

pace, nudging a floe here and there, watching them dance to a slow, secret tune played by the currents.

Hour after hour we nosed, but Cape Byrd, our immediate objective, seemed as far away as ever and the concentration of ice around the ship worsened. Commands to the engine room: 'dead-slow' 'stop' 'dead slow astern' were coming in rapid succession. The compressed air bottles, used for throwing in the clutch, were being used incessantly. By early afternoon, the ship was surrounded by hundreds of ice-floes, some 200 yards across. Open water was tantalisingly close but we were hedged in on every quarter, and Jim said: 'A bit trickier than I thought Wilks. Better get Ken up and start the evacuation procedure.'

We were in the sort of floes which had fatally pinched the Southern Quest a year ago, not a few miles from where we were. And she had been an ice-strengthened vessel. Our flimsy hull would accept only the slightest pressure. I asked Ken to estimate the weight of some of the bigger floes. 'A few thousand tons, I guess,' he said.

Two of the crew pushed floes away from the stern with boat hooks. I hung over the bow, shouting distances to the next so Jim could gauge commands to give the engine room. Davey Edward suddenly appeared on

'Well done, Jim!' We finally round Cape Bird at the second attempt (left to right) Pete Wilkinson, Ken Ballard, Irmi Mussack, Xavier Pastor, Hannah Sorensen, Nolan Loveridge, Jim Cottier, Justin Farralley *(Loor/Greenpeace)*.

the bridge in a temper, sweating from the heat of the engine room, his overalls smeared with grease and oil.

'What the fuck's going on?' he demanded. 'We've made hundreds of manoeuvres in the past five hours. We're running out of air. We can't keep this up!'

He looked beyond Jim to the ice.

'Fucking hell' he said quietly, 'I think I'll get below.'

The evacuation was underway. It was non-essential people first, which didn't include me, or Davey Edwards. The journalists and film crew, sensing a big story, were beside themselves with indignation as they boarded the helicopters in the first wave of evacuees. Inch by inch, Jim pushed back towards the clear water we had left that morning. By late evening, we were free. I worded a press release playing down the drama. Despite its mild nature, the predictable press calls asked 'how long have you been stuck in the ice?', 'does this mean you're calling the expedition off?'

Two days later, we tried again – and made it. For the first time, we saw Cape Byrd from just a few hundred yards away, and as we entered the ice-free water of McMurdo Sound I walked into the saloon and did a mad, ecstatic jig around the room with Kevin Conaglen, our base-leader.

Tempests and blizzards notwithstanding, we would build our base, and Greenpeace would install a wintering team for the first ever year-round protest in the Antarctic. Jim and I shook hands on the foredeck in

front of cameras. I could have squeezed the breath out of Jim in my joy.
Jim said, 'That was the easy bit Wilks. Now we've work to do.'

14. At Sea Again

My first sight of Cape Evans will stay with me forever.

I gazed at the scene speechless. It was overcast weather, and snow was driven horizontally before a stiff wind. I came up on the bridge as we were about to anchor 300 yards offshore. My eyes were confronted by a black, gently sloping beach no more than 100 yards deep before the terrain rose to the hills and hummocks of Ross Island. Every child in England is steeped in the history of Scott of the Antarctic, and to the right of me was Scott's historic hut. I had studied pictures of it and read and re-read in awe the tragic story of his bid for the South Pole in 1910. The hut looked as though it could have been built yesterday, so slow is the process of deterioration in the Antarctic.

We made the short trip in an inflatable dinghy. Stepping ashore I grabbed a fistful of the black gravel and made an inane comment for the

'Here stood my childhood hero.' Pete Wilkinson stands mesmerised outside Scott's Hut at Cape Evans *(Keith Swenson)*.

cameras. Then I made my way in a mesmeric state to the hut. I stood on the very spot where Oates, Evans, Bowers, Cherry-Garrard, Wilson and Scott himself had struggled, toiled, laughed and fought, more than 70 years before in what Scott himself described as 'this awful place'.

Scott's rubbish was scattered all around. Tins, food boxes, wire, boots, wood and even the oats upon which the sacrificial and totally unsuited ponies were fed, lay all around. It seems that he had as little regard for the vulnerability of the Antarctic as do the contemporary conquistadors.

It was time for work. The ship had to be discharged of its 150 tons of equipment, and the Greenpeace Base built. We had a mammoth amount of material to shift in a few short weeks, and we had also agreed to bring back the gear, including the Cessna aeroplane, which had been left by the Footsteps of Scott expedition a year before. It was now early January and we would have to leave within five weeks. Temperatures were -10°C. With luck they would rise, but by late February they would be -20°C and lower. Within the space of a day, the sea could be covered with a thin film, heralding the return of the thicker sea ice and the cruel Antarctic winter. We had to work fast and pray that blizzards would not shorten the time available to us.

The weather held. Only three days were lost due to white-outs when we couldn't see from one end of the ship to the other, let alone to the shore. Swirling snow squalls, coupled with low cloud and mist, arrived with frightening speed. Anyone going aloft or ashore had to sign out with the bridge where a log was kept of crew movement. No-one ventured out except with emergency survival gear.

As material left the ship, lifted by the helicopter from the aft-deck, we could see the hut taking shape on shore. Eventually, the last of the wall-panels made their short journey and were bolted to the floor sections, then the roof panels. Ken strutted round deck speaking in inaudible grunts to the pilot and crane operators through his headset, 'Yoooouuuupppp. . . .' was a typical command and could have meant anything. At the same time he would be blithely waving at us deck-hands in gestures incomprehensible to anyone who hadn't worked with him for months. When the roof was on, there was a short celebration, which we ship-bound personnel enviously watched through binoculars. 'Barrels' came Ken's grunt. It was time for the back-breaking task of off-loading 250 barrels of fuel which would power the generators throughout the year.

Off came the hatch covers and into the cramped holds jumped the deckies to struggle with barrels weighing 200 kilos each. They were rolled beneath the open hatch cover, lifted two at a time by the crane and rolled to the aft deck. The helicopter was fired up and the mildly terrifying task of 'hooking on' was allocated.

The helicopter clattered straight at us, hooks trailing beneath. We had

Sling-loading: a terrifying task during which lives were in the hands of the skilfull pilots demonstrating the art of precision flying *(Morgan/Greenpeace)*.

to grab the hooks as the chopper hovered only a few feet above, and untangle and attach them to the lip of the barrels. Then we'd roll out two more, chock them and wait for the return of the helicopter. Daily, we entrusted our lives to the precision flying and immense skill of our pilots. The noise was deafening, even with ear-protectors. An added hazard was the build up of static electricity on the hooks. As you grabbed one, electricity was discharged through the body, often severely. Ken had once seen a seaman thrown 20 feet from such a shock, and so the pilots would earth the chains on the deck rail before we grabbed them, or we'd whack them with a lump of wood to clear the static charge.

We were also in Antarctica to monitor activities at the giant US base 15 miles away at McMurdo, and draw attention to environmental transgressions. To those ends, we made our official visits. The US and indeed New Zealand personnel, from the nearby Scott Base, regularly dumped redundant machines and scrap metal onto ice to await the thaw and the disappearance of the rubbish into the depths of McMurdo Sound. It is estimated that 'several thousand tons' of scrap metal and machinery were disposed off in this way over the years. We photographed the evidence and pumped the pictures to the world, amid growing US antipathy to our presence.

The tricky task of lifting the fuselage of the Cessna with the helicopter had long been looked forward to by the crew. Grace O'Sullivan, a very experienced deckhand and skilled driver, brought the wings of the plane over on the inflatable, one at a time. Ken, John Welsh and I, responsible for stowing the parts on deck, had manoeuvred the port-side wing to its stowage position when I blithely stepped into an open hold and fell ten feet, luckily onto a pile of cardboard boxes. As the weeks wore on, tiredness and wandering concentration became our worst enemies.

The closer we came to completing the job, the tetchier and more exhausted people became. Mid-February arrived and temperatures dropped fast. Stamina waned dangerously and we worked against the clock in the icy blast of the Antarctic wind. It became harder to drag ourselves from the warmth of our bunks, more of a chore to don the heavy Antarctic clothing and harder to forsake the civility of the mess where there were

Here we go, here we go, here we go! The Greenpeace navy and airforce leaves Auckland for Antarctica on the 3rd December 1988 *(Morgan/ Greenpeace)*.

plates of fried egg and bacon and steaming mugs of tea.

At last the operation was complete. When the time came to sail, we said emotional farewells to the overwintering team, knowing that this time we had achieved all the targets we had set ourselves. We said good-bye to our four good friends who would act as watchdogs for Greenpeace throughout the long Antarctic winter.

The familiar, dreaded knock on the door, Werner's gentle voice calling me to take my steering watch, the mumbled reply. Then the instant assessment of the state of the sea and, more critically, the state of my stomach. Worst of all, the glance in the mirror as I stumble across the pitching cabin for the door. Could that be me, staring back, hair on end, eyes set in darkened sockets, at sea again with Greenpeace?

I make it to the bridge and thankfully my stomach takes only a few minutes to adjust, abating the feeling of nausea to one of mild discomfort. The 4-8 watch are going off for breakfast in jovial mood. We exchange the normal insults as eight bells sound. I feel the familiar rush of adrenaline as we head for Antarctica for the fourth time in a newly acquired ship. It is 1988. I am determined it is to be my last expedition. Southwards, ever southwards.

We had gone back to Antarctica a third time, still in the m.v. Greenpeace.

We had replaced the scientists who had spent their year monitoring the US base, collecting data and conducting experiments for Greenpeace, as well as pursuing personal projects. After re-supplying the base, we had sailed and flown around the coast documenting the environmental nightmares which the majority of bases perpetrated blatantly. Then once again, we had made our long voyage home.

On the outward journey of this fourth voyage, I was in a state of excitement for new reasons. One was that we were finally using a ship suitable for the Antarctic, an ice-strengthened vessel dubbed Gondwana. Moreover, Greenpeace International had quietly announced that we could flex our direct-action muscles at last. No longer irresponsible novices, we had moved from disastrous beginnings to smooth, well-equipped professionalism, and were now at liberty to translate direct-action expertise into the Antarctic arena. We had catalogued and documented long enough. This was what many of us had been waiting for.

Months of gruelling planning prior to departure from Auckland had laid the groundwork. We would exchange overwinterers and resupply the base as usual – but first we had three actions up our sleeves; against the Japanese whaling fleet; a blockade of the French airstrip at Dumont D'Urville; and a pipe-blocking action in the giant US base at McMurdo, where cadmium waste poured non-stop into Winterquarters Bay.

I had established a regular Friday night meeting in the skipper's cabin at which we went over and over, again and again, the details for our planned actions, and sought new angles. Whackier and whackier ideas were encouraged by a case of beer provided for the occasion.

With Henk Haazen, the big, burly Dutchman in charge of logistics, I constantly checked the inventory for the trip, testing him, asking him to trot out his deadlines and progress. With Ken Ballard, I went over equipment lists, deadlines, routes, dates and sea times between locations, and the likelihood of meeting the whalers. With the TV crew and photographer I went over itineraries, photo outlines, routines we would be implementing, helicopter time and picture transmission procedures. The ship was alive and humming to the throb of a crew in tune with the task ahead and the myriad jobs in hand.

This time I had a co-campaigner on board, an American. Paul Bogart and I had met the previous year in Washington, and become friends immediately. He was nicknamed Doglips (Dog for short) and was droll, unflappable and extremely sharp, an excellent campaigner and an invaluable partner. We were hoping for good press coverage but things, as usual, were very much in the lap of the gods.

Nothing could have prepared us for the massive attention this trip was to attract, and no-one could have predicted how lucky we would be. Though we did get off to a very bad start. Mine particularly was inauspicious.

A few nights before we left, I dunned it into the crew that we were all ambassadors for Greenpeace. We should be on our best behaviour when ashore. By 3am, I had been thrown out of a nightclub, threatened a bouncer, and the police were looking for me all over port.

I was ribbed mercilessly by the chortling crew. Then in the bunkering dock taking on fuel later that day, one of the pipes developed an air-lock. 50 litres of fuel spilled on deck and, before we could stop it, much of it had escaped through the scuppers. Although it was a minor spill, any amount of oil on water spreads rapidly and widely. As the ship's crew undertook dispersal operations from the dinghies, we reported the accident to the Harbour Master. Within minutes, the quayside was swarming with press. 'Greenpeace pollutes harbour!' was a typical banner headline. Years later, to my amazement, a *Guardian* cross-word clue read: 'Ship which leaked oil in harbour while en route to oil exploration protest in Antarctica?'

We sailed on an evening tide. The picture of Munch's Scream was taken down from the cabin we had used as an office and which Henk had nick-named 'The Nervous Centre'. I revelled in the luxury of a single cabin, my first in all my years of going to sea with Greenpeace in six different vessels. I had even, on Ken's suggestion, spent $100 in Auckland on a Lazy Boy reclining chair which, although it cluttered the cabin and took up most of the limited floor space, became the envy of the ship. It allowed me to sit in a reclining position to alleviate the worst effects of seasickness. With Christmas cards and good-will messages plastered over the cabin and my sound system wired up, I had a private bolt-hole to retreat to, where I could play whatever music I liked without worrying about the preferences of a cabin-mate.

We slipped into the familiar routines of a ship at sea. Once or twice a week as we ploughed south, the video addicts watched one movie after another. On other more socially amiable evenings, a party would break out with much drinking and dancing. These proceedings were interrupted from time to time by crew meetings at which Dog and I would again go over arrangements for the first landfall.

We steamed first for the French base, Dumont D'Urville, on Point Geologie. Here our old enemies were blasting a fragile and ecologically important archipelago, home to 75,000 penguins and other seabirds, to construct an airstrip – in the name of science, of course. Perversely, they had originally built their base here in order to study the very birds whose nesting sites they were now blasting to smithereens.

While rock-blasting was taking place, the penguins would be rounded up and held in pens. When the penguins were released they would invariably return to sit pathetically on the exact spot where their nest had been. The French insisted that their activities were having little impact on breeding rates and were proving their concern by replacing real eggs with plastic ones, hoping that the poor birds would move away to a more productive place when these didn't hatch.

Our intention was to delay work on the airstrip for as long as possible during the brief summer weeks available to the construction team, and to harm their operation financially. We hoped we could get the work postponed a year – when we would come back again to continue the disruption.

We planned to block the partly built runway with a survival hut, secured by stakes driven into the permafrost. We hoped to occupy the hut, known as an Apple, for up to three weeks. Of course, we were sufficiently familiar with French reactions to Greenpeace to know they would not simply put their feet up and wait for us to leave. But we were ill-prepared for the ferocity of their response to our tactics.

Two days out from Dumont D'Urville, we entered into the round of diplomacy, usual before any action. We lodged an official complaint and gave warning of our intention to demonstrate. The base leader, M. Hussein, accepted our faxed messages with courtesy and acknowledged our opposition. He invited us to the base for an 'official' meeting. It was going to be an interesting few weeks at DuDu, as we called it for short.

The archipelago of Pointe Geologie was littered with lorries, diggers, dumpers and other heavy machinery. The cries of the penguins vied with engines and drilling machines. A helicopter droned overhead. We launched the inflatables and nosed our way through ice-floes to the landing platform. Hussein greeted us with a smile. We spoke French as well as my limited knowledge would allow, with Pierette Paroz, our Swiss helicopter pilot, interpreting when I could not manage.

Hussein's brave attempt at defending the airstrip, quoting irrelevant reports and meaningless statistics, triggered my more aggressive side, even in poor French.

'Look round you,' I said. 'You're operating bulldozers, blasting rock and dumping tons of material into the sea in the middle of a penguin colony, and you say there's no impact! That's bullshit, and you know it. We begin the protest within 48 hours.'

Back on board, we prepared the Apple, checked the banner and placards and lifted them into an inflatable ready for launching in the morning. Then we checked through our plans again. We would move to the airstrip first thing, and hold the banner across the width of the work area. I hoped they would let us get on with this unmolested, thinking that was all we were up to.

I overslept and a tetchy Ken shook me roughly.

'Get up you lazy sod! Everyone's waiting.'

The inflatables were already in the water, and the first wave of protesters headed off as I came on deck. We clambered ashore with our banner and placards, and the press corps fanned out to capture the demonstration on film. Henk, who had been on the Rainbow Warrior in Auckland Harbour when the French sank her, suggested we wait a little, until as many vehicles as possible had entered the cul-de-sac of the airstrip. Then we could move across to block their exit. When three dumpers were on the spit of land between us and the end of the runway, we spread out and unfurled the banner. The drivers returned from their dumping run, nosed up to our thin line of protesters, switched off and stalked past, muttering 'fou' and 'merde'. They watched us with ill-disguised scorn as we stood there having our pictures taken, feeling rather trivial. But behind us, the ruse was working. Henk and Ken were struggling unseen to get the hut sections up a six foot scree. Soon the second wave of people were ashore putting it together. We needed fifteen minutes.

The hut grew in shape. Finally it was up and occupied, and we moved the banner away. Sitting smack in the middle of their beautiful runway was our gleaming Apple. Inside and busily making it habitable, were five Greenpeace people. We had a good proportion of their hardware behind our barricade. They couldn't work on this southerly section of the airstrip, where some of their vehicles were stranded.

I sauntered over to Dog with a smile of relief, and Sean Lesley, the cameraman, zoomed in on our conversation. I asked Dog what he thought and his answer was immortalised on film:

'I think we got 'em by the balls.'

And, for the moment, we had.

15. DuDu

The tranquillity of the afternoon, as we basked in brilliant sunshine at Dumont D'urville, was only disturbed by the now distant thump of machinery working away to our north. We revelled in the peace we had managed to bring. The penguins seemed to appreciate it too, and rediscovered their long-lost bravado, making forays to the hut.

Henk was lying asleep on his back outside, directly in the path of an on-coming penguin strutting his comical way up the strip. On reaching Henk's sizeable bulk, the penguin stopped and then hopped up onto him. Henk opened a quizzical eye and the penguin took two short hops across

Royal protester joins the airstrip occupation at Dumont D'Urville: Emperor penguin on the piste *(Morgan/ Greenpeace).*

his stomach and jumped down the other side.

But the peace and humour were soon to be disturbed in a big way.

The distant clanking of machinery grew louder. Around the corner came what looked like a lynch mob, either side of a huge digging machine with a jagged-toothed bucket fixed to its hydraulic arm. Leading the ensemble was the head of the construction team, a tank of a man called Engler. He demanded the release of his vehicles, on the pretext that he was responsible for their maintenance and that leaving them unattended in the cold Antarctic weather would cause them to freeze up. I told him we were responsible for the environment and would not move.

He replied, 'C'est domage' – and waved his infantry forward.

There followed a free-for-all in which they dragged us from the Apple and attempted to pin us down forcibly. Machinery began to move forward and bodies flew left, right and centre. We had not planned for this eventuality. As I was dragged from beneath the wheels of a dumper truck, at the same time hanging on for grim death to Werner's legs, I mentally kicked myself for the oversight. I snuck a look at Henk, standing his ground stubbornly while three of them attempted to topple him to the ground.

The last truck squeezed by the hut, dislodging it from its moorings, amid cheers from the French. Henk, Paul and others followed the retreating men down the strip jibing and taunting them. To my consternation, Dog seemed as if he were unable to pack up.

'Come on, come on, Frenchie. Come and get some of this, assole.'

I put my arm around his waist and led him back to the battered hut where people were brushing themselves down, brewing up tea and rolling cigarettes. I walked over to the photographer and cameraman.

'Did you get it, guys?'

'Everything. But shit, you only just stuck to the 'peaceful' part of your name!' said Sean.

I was back on board ship within the hour, pumping out the press release and a selection of photos. Looking at the contact sheets, I could see what Sean meant. We had been subjected to severe provocation, but in several of the photos, it was the French guys getting the heave-ho. In one, our cook was taking a well-aimed kick at a retreating back. I began to worry whether people like Henk, who were scarred forever by that July night in Auckland harbour, could continue the protest without retaliating. I didn't trust myself all that much either.

My fears were reinforced by a visit to my cabin from Paul Brown, a *Guardian* journalist travelling with us, for whom I had (and have) great respect. He was quite shaken by the events of the afternoon, and counselled me to secure an agreement with Hussein which would prevent the escalation of violence from both sides.

I commuted between ship and the party occupying the hut to keep everyone abreast of events. Press calls were coming in at every hour of the day and night, and Dog and I took shifts to deal with them. The Greenpeace empire was also jamming lines, concerned for our safety, but I played everything down for fear some directive might arrive to stop us. We had a running story here but I was anxious to direct attention to the issue of the airstrip, not the aggression. I wired off faxes to the French Antarctic Division in Paris protesting at the causes of our concern.

Tensions were increasing. Over the years the festering feud between Greenpeace and the French had refused to go away. They had rammed our ships, bombarded us with tear-gas and stun-grenade canisters, used riot police and dogs on protestors, sunk the beloved Warrior and murdered Fernando. The following day someone suggested we remove the name Greenpeace from all our equipment and finally have it out with them. Much as many of us dearly would have liked to, we concentrated our attention instead on the northern end of the airstrip.

With work at the southern end at a standstill because of our blockade, the French continued to work on the northern end of the runway. We decided to occupy the slopes down which 12-ton loads of rock were dumped into the sea, extending the runway. To be effective we had to do this while work was going on and it was extremely hazardous to ourselves. But the French didn't bat an eyelid. Huge boulders careered past vulnerable flesh time after time, until someone finally thought better of it. They then began to dump their loads at the end of the runway instead, leaving the boulders to be bulldozed over the edge at a later date. We moved our protest too, and stood beneath their skips as they were jacked vertical by the hydraulic ram. As the skips rose higher into the air, the rocks would shift and settle momentarily and we would duck out of the way. Henk would not budge as the movement of rocks began, and was deaf to our pleas to him; time after time we had to drag him away at the last moment.

Suddenly the Gondwana sounded its claxon, and I made radio contact. They had received a frantic call from the party occupying the Apple on the other end of the strip, saying they were under attack and needed immediate assistance. Ken, waiting in the inflatable ten yards off-shore, roared in to collect us. We sped round to the southern end of the strip to see the hut being dragged from its position by a digger. Scenes similar to those of the previous day were in progress. The French had smashed a hole in the side of the hut to remove everyone, because the ship's electrician had blocked the entrance by chaining himself across it.

Watching this from the dinghy, we hurled a broadside of abuse at the French. As the nose of the inflatable hit the bottom of the scree, we cleared six feet of rubble and made for the hut. I was seized as I ran, but the

'Bundle!' Wilkinson (bottom left) and other Greenpeace protesters are unceremoniously dragged out of the path of vehicles trapped behind their
barricade *(Morgan/Greenpeace)*.

horizontal figure of Ken Ballard took out both my captors in a two-armed
rugby tackle. He dragged me from the ground and propelled me towards
the hut. Henk had reached the door and was wrestling his way through an
army of workers who seemed to bounce off him. We hurled ourselves
inside as the Apple was dragged along the stony surface.

We lay in a panting, sweaty heap on the floor inside the hut, exhausted,
elated and laughing uncontrollably. We had reclaimed it, though its value
as a survival hut had been ruined. A gaping hole created by French boots
yawned in one of the panels. We wearily pushed the Apple the hundred
yards back to its original position. Henk set to work repairing it while I
photographed from every angle, evidence for any legal actions we might
take: it had escaped my mind that this was as lawless a place as the old
Wild West.

The demands of pumping out news of this latest skirmish could not
wait. Dog and I went back to the ship and began work on the press release. We were wiped out. Dog offered to write the first draft on the computer while I showered and sank a beer. An hour later, I found him in the
radio room, staring at a blank screen. In that hour, he had managed to
write, 'The international environmental organisation, Greenpeace. . . .'

'Sorry, Wilks. Give it a go will you?'

'Go and suss out the pix with Steve – and think of captions!'

I sat and stared at Paul's intro. This was the eighth release we had put out and I knew it would prompt a flood of calls which would have us both up till all hours. I went below and rounded up Paul and Steve. 'Let's have a night off,' I suggested. 'The world can wait.' We had a few beers, then wrote and sent the release.

I knew we had to cool down. The atmosphere of anarchy and violence was at boiling point. Dog and I toyed with the idea of offering an olive branch. We would occupy the southern end of the strip and forget the northern end in return for a guarantee of no further violence and, most importantly, the French must allow us time to make a sensible assessment of the impact the airstrip was having. Paul Brown arrived back on board after interviewing Engler. Engler had told Brown that if the protesters wanted to commit suicide, that was their prerogative. The airstrip would not be delayed. Paul had asked if this policy would be adhered to even if serious injury or a death was the price. Engler repeated his statement. The wisdom of reducing the opportunities for violent confrontation was confirmed.

As expected, our news releases prompted a flood of inquiries: CNN, AAP, ABC, Australian newspapers and even German media called repeatedly. In between the calls, we spent the morning in deep discussion with those on board and with the shore party, trying to convince them that we should turn down the heat. We finally agreed we would strike the Apple a few days early in return for our stated conditions.

All was quiet ashore: Hussein had declared a day of rest to 'allow tempers to cool', and those occupying the hut were left alone. That evening he called to say that Paris wanted us out even sooner than we were suggesting. But they did offer us, in return, a day of 'scientific evaluation' to assess the impact of the airstrip. It was a great break, though Henk, Ken and a few others felt we were selling out. Later, fifteen people crowded into Ken's tiny cabin and the position of a bottle of rum helped soothe their disappointment.

We moved ashore to dismantle our brave little Apple, taking a final celebration picture, and poured champagne which Pat King, the cook, had been keeping for a special occasion. Paul Bogart, Liz Carr (one of the wintering scientists) and the more interested crew joined the French scientists and our press entourage to wander round Dumont D'Urville for an examination of whether a building site in the middle of 75,000 breeding penguins could be judged environmentally friendly. I declined to join them. The answer was obvious. We were to sail that evening. We slowly drove the loaded inflatables back across mirror-smooth, sparkling waters. The shore party returned during the afternoon.

Before leaving, we took the inflatables out for a last look at Point Geologie. We nosed into nooks and crannies of the little islands on the archipelago which still awaited their fate, and switched off engines. We watched the antics of the penguins for an hour. It was quite the most beautiful memory I treasure. For a while, we could shut out the noise and mayhem which human beings bring, and feast our eyes on a scene unchanged in over a thousand years.

I got to the party going on in Henk's cabin around 1am and he engulfed me in his burly arms, breathing rum as he planted a big kiss on my forehead.

'Wilks,' he said, 'You're an assole, but you're the best.'

We were steaming into the teeth of a force 7, but I slept like a baby.

One press release too far. 'Doglips' Bogart rethinks strategy in the saloon of the Gondwana *(Steve Morgan)*.

16. Biscuits

Thoughts turned to the Japanese whaling fleet, out there somewhere in 160,000 square miles of ocean. Finding them would be a near impossibility. Meantime we had other visits to make.

Commonwealth Bay lay on our route. Ken ordered the boats to be lowered amongst stunning icebergs and the bleak backdrop of the Antarctic coastline. Seals and penguins basked in their hundreds on flat rocks sloping gently into the sea, as we tramped across a snowfield 500 yards wide. Here, 80 years ago, my biggest Antarctic hero had built his hut out of the keening wind before setting off on an expedition during which he lost both his companions and suffered privations beyond belief.

Douglas Mawson's hut was maintained by the Australians. Its timbers gleamed from the scouring they received from wind-blown grit. Bitter winds of two hundred miles an hour are not uncommon at this, the windiest spot on earth. All around, as at Scott's hut, was an incredible clutter of rubbish – boots, tin cans, wire, wood, a fallen aerial pole, wooden crates and the dross of human passing.

Even if I could find it in my heart to forgive Mawson for this disrespectful scene, I could do no such thing for the maintenance team whose recent rubbish of ring-pull cans and modern-day containers added to the mess. People really did see the Antarctic as one gigantic rubbish tip. I moved away to watch the penguins and blot out this antipathy I felt towards my fellow human beings. As I wandered over the rocks, carefully avoiding the moss beds and lichens where the imprint of a foot will stay ten years, so slow is the metabolic rate, I noticed the decaying remains of many penguins trapped in a crevass between the rocks. What a death these poor creatures must have suffered, dying of hunger and freezing as their helpless fellows looked on. The unforgiving Antarctic wind moaned at me around the headland, and I tried to imagine this place in the depths of a winter storm, when light would not penetrate for months.

We visited the Soviet Base at Leningradskaya, the Italian base at Terra Nova, and the German base at Gondwana, always receiving tremendous welcomes and hospitality despite the work we did. These many outposts in Antarctica have been established in pursuit of science, but also so that their governments can lay 'legitimate' claims to real estate when the land eventually yields up its long-hidden riches.

At the Russian base, reached after a nerve-racking 65-mile helicopter flight, old vehicles poked through the ice like decaying teeth. Rubbish was everywhere round the base, which itself seemed precariously perched on a steep cliff. The many 'seals' we had seen on the ice far below as we flew over turned out to be thousands of empty fuel barrels, casually pitched over the cliff when finished with. But if they were environmentally backward, the hospitality and friendship of the Russians was unsurpassed.

We had to haul questions through three languages – Russian, then German, then English – a three-way translation. An early question: 'Beer now, eat and tour later, or tour now, eat and beer later, or eat now, tour and then beer?' became so confused that the base commander decided we needed a few warming vodkas while the momentous decision was made. We took away our inspection notes and photo-documentation for submission to the Antarctic Treaty Parties and weaved our way unsteadily back to the helicopter; warm with friendship, gifts and endearing memories.

Unusually, we had visited this base without any of the press corps and film crew. This had angered me, because we would lack a movie record of the terrible state of the Soviet Base. Intrepid as ever, though, Paul Brown and Steve Morgan, our stills photographer, braved the long and potentially dangerous flight and duly filed their story.

At the German camp we were greeted by two Antarctic enthusiasts of the first order. These geologists had only a small survival hut. It stood on stilts on a piece of high ground, and before it they had pitched two small tents. They stored their provisions in the hut and lived in the tents, so keen were they to experience the Antarctic 'in the raw'. These thoroughly likeable guys could not walk past a rock without stopping to relate its age, its origin and how it came to be there. It was fascinating, and we sat in their provision-cluttered hut for two hours. Their colleagues were in North Victorialand, mapping the continental coast to determine where Tasmania had once fitted into it like a huge jigsaw piece before breaking away and drifting to more temperate climes. I could have listened all night, but sadly Ken called on the VHF to warn us of deteriorating weather.

As we flew in the direction of the Gondwana in a gathering snowstorm, pilot Dave Walley asked disconcertingly:

'Anyone see the ship?'

Each time we made our dream-like journeys over the skin of this truly amazing land, the sight of the ship, red hull against a seemingly unending spread of ice, was sobering. This tiny speck of metal was all there was between us and the harsh and perilous nature of the Antarctic.

Gondwana was a floating bulldozer. She elbowed most floes out of her way with consummate ease. As we dug further and further south, however, progress became slower. We decided to make straight for Ross Island and exchange our overwinterers before trying to find the whalers; if we did find them, it would be a potential bonus on our way home.

Naoko Funawashi, our Japanese journalist and interpreter, was objecting to the banners we had prepared – 'Stop the bloody (scientific) whaling' which translates roughly into Japanese as 'Stop being barbarians'. She felt the Japanese press would find this racist.

The 23rd January was my mother's birthday and I placed a satellite telephone call, eating up my three minutes monthly allowance. By that afternoon the ship had once again begun to dance to the tune of the open ocean. We'd been virtually ice-bound for weeks, and the movement saw many heading for their bunks. We rounded the knuckle of the north-western tip of the Ross Sea coast and began to make headway. As I sat preparing updates for the Greenpeace empire during the afternoon, Albert Kuichen, the huge mountain of a Dutch mate, came silently up behind me and whispered,

'Wilks, there's a ship on the horizon. Could be a whaler, eh?'

'Albert, get outta here. You serious?'

'She's there OK, mate.' He winked and I was left wondering if he really meant it.

Curiosity got the better of me. I went to the bridge and found all the mates and the skipper training binoculars on a distant speck. She was seven miles away. Whaling vessels have a distinctive look – high bow sweeping away dramatically to a gunwale which gives almost no freeboard. From this distance, it was hard to tell, but she was closing on us quickly. Suddenly, there on the radar screen were two more small echoes and a large, fat, juicy one. It could only be the 40,000-ton floating abattoir, the Nishin Maru.

We had almost literally bumped into the Japanese fleet. Within minutes, the bridge was swamped by bleary-eyed crew fresh from their bunks, hugging each other, staring and chattering in a cacophony of disbelief. I went to rouse Sean, Tim and Steve Morgan, the film and photo crew on board. Then we sat tight and awaited their first moves. No helicopters, no radio contact yet – just wait and see.

The whale catcher we had first sighted was clearly visible now, its high bow cleaving the chill waters with disdain. Whalers are graceful vessels: if only their purpose weren't so odious, they would have been a delight to watch. They were fast too, reaching 17 knots flat out, far faster than the Gondwana.

We changed course surreptitiously. I asked Ian the radio operator, and Naoko, if there were any chance of intercepting their radio traffic. Within minutes, Ian was back up the stairs:

'Wilks, Quick! We started scanning and tuned into the first Japanese sounding chatter. And it's them! They're saying 'if it's Greenpeace we'll try to out-run them'. Oh shit, this is incredible!'

We closed quickly, but she didn't run immediately. Like two boxers sizing each other up, we circled, the Nishin Maru's rails full to brimming with aproned workers peering at us.

Naoko came to the bridge to speak to the Nishin Maru. Their chief scientist said they had caught 40 whales so far in what he called a scientific mission.

The Nishin hove to for the night, and so did we, though under cover of darkness we crept closer. As I came on watch the following morning, we were in the bang and crash of a full-bloodied chase, trailing the Nishin Maru by about a mile. The wind was picking up and the seas growing steeper all the time. The Nishin Maru's skipper was testing our endurance and determination. As we bucked and rolled across the ocean, our ship became a battlefield of broken crockery, spilled liquids, prone bodies and the pervading smell of human vomit. Through all this Dog and I fed the press and picked up the calls which resulted. It is one of the most thankless jobs on a Greenpeace vessel: sounding cheerful, enthusiastic and articulate, with your stomach in an express lift gone haywire. After a two-day chase, the Nishin Maru rendezvoused with the whale catchers. The hunt was to resume.

The Japanese fleet assembled into hunting configuration. From the bridge, I looked aft to see our inflatables being prepared for launching. The catchers moved faster than we could, but they would have to slow down when they began to hunt in earnest. The tell-tale spouts from fleeing whales showed that this would not be long.

Ken called me to the main deck and indicated with a flick of his eyes that I was to drive the crane. It was the heavy aluminium workboat he wanted in the water first. I dropped the 1-ton boat as the Gondwana bucked on the swell, and the engines roared into life. She was away, with Henk at the controls. The inflatables followed.

The Greenpeace navy was off on a charge across the choppy seas. From the bridge, I watched through binoculars. The helicopter clattered overhead with Sean and Steve hanging out of the spaces where the doors should have been, cameras at the ready. Ken, Henk and the others were about to use themselves as human shields between the whales and 200-kilo exploding harpoons travelling at 60 mph.

One whaler was about to fire. As she slid from view behind an iceberg, Ken and Henk swept into position beneath her bow. We waited with bated breath for them to emerge on the other side. The factory ship had slowed too, and the Gondwana puffed up to the centre of the hunt. Arne, our skipper, whacked the throttles forward on the Gondwana and attempted to head off a whalecatcher on our port side. Whales spouted all around. As the vessel came alongside, kicking spray up into huge sheets, Japanese lookouts refused to acknowledge our presence and she passed with only feet separating us. She lined up on her quarry. Arne honked the claxon

Ken Ballard postions his inflatable between the whale and whaler in classic Greenpeace protest action, Southern Ocean, 1989 *(Morgan/Greenpeace)*.

for all he was worth, the crew lined the guard rails and then 'BANG!' The dull thud of the explosion momentarily concussed our ears. From the bow, someone screamed, 'Missed!'

As the whaler veered away, Arne brought the Gondwana alongside again and tried to force her off course. But a second whale blew right beneath the whaler's bow, and this time he didn't miss. The whale sounded deeply as the harpoon exploded inside it, and the hawser between it and the catcher went taut. The winch on the catcher whirred: the whale was being hauled back to a miserable and lingering death. As the whale surfaced, we stopped to film.

It quivered from head to tail, its mouth opening and closing, blood spilling into the sea. It was winched in tightly beneath the catcher's bow, and two electrodes attached. This seemed to increase its agony, and it thrashed around in ever weakening attempts at escape until, at last, it was still.

The sea was stained with its blood. Maggie McCaw, our forceful American deckie, turned to me sobbing and I comforted her as best I could. The whale was secured alongside the catcher, its head beneath the waterline while the boat steamed sluggishly towards the factory ship a few hundred yards away. Its death had taken about fifteen minutes. As the carcass was transferred to the slipway on the bigger boat, I realised the operation was most vulnerable at this point. If we could position ourselves almost on the stern ramp of the factory ship, a whale could not be transferred. A catcher encumbered by a whale it could not discharge, could not hunt.

The tiny 6-ton whale was dragged up the slipway built in the 1930s to accommodate 100-ton carcasses of blue and fin whales. The minke looked so insignificant on that vast expanse. Blood poured from blow-hole, mouth and wound; another tiny indelible stain on the collective conscience of humankind. On board the Gondwana, the mood was sombre.

The afternoon was spent dogging one catcher after another. It was exhilarating work. Albert the mate got it off to a fine art and, on more than one occasion, the catchers had to veer away for fear of a collision. Throughout the day we kept at it, restricting the catch to two whales.

On the bridge the following morning, I called the camera teams together with Arne, the mates and Dog, to plan the day's activities. We would stick firmly to the factory ship to prevent her accepting dead whales. Fortunately the Gondwana was highly manoeuvrable. Getting within 20 yards of a 40,000 tonner on the high seas is not accepted maritime behaviour, but it presented no real danger to either vessel.

A catcher arrived with a carcass and Arne timed his run to perfection, arriving only metres from the factory vessel's stern. Unable to approach, the catcher had to lay off and fume. Arne stuck to his position doggedly.

Arne Sorensen stations the Gondwana hard on the stern of the factory vessel to prevent the transfer of whales from the catchers *(Morgan/ Greenpeace)*.

The skipper of the Nishin Maru called on the VHF and demanded that we leave him two miles of sea room. That had us rolling with laughter.

The catcher's skipper was furious and yelled out all manner of abuse from the bridge, before coming in for another run. As he slowed alongside the Gondwana, he drifted closer and closer. His superstructure was inches from our rubbing strake and then we touched with a jolt. Paul Brown immediately pulled out his note book and wrote, 'Greenpeace and catcher ship collide in mid ocean at 1823 local time.' One tabloid in the UK reported we were sinking.

Our heavy work-boat was fitted with a custom-made banner which we put in front of a catcher for a few hours to continue the harassment. Even the helicopter was pressed into service trailing a banner from a weighted wire which dangled over the harpoon on the bow. We wanted to disrupt their operations as widely as possible and make them anxious about our versatility. We also wanted them to think we were prepared to stay indefinitely. In reality we were running out of time.

Only 13 whales had been loaded since we had joined the fleet. They had taken 40 in a similar period before we arrived. Now we relied on the Greenpeace network and the public, to use what we had done to best effect. They didn't fail us: Japanese Embassies got hit around the world. To our great delight, the British put a resolution to the International Whaling Commission demanding that this particular operation 'be abandoned immediately.' Over ten days we had exposed 'scientific' whaling for what it was – merely commercial whaling in another guise with exactly the same results: dead whales and whalemeat on the menu at fancy Japanese restaurants.

There was one last act to play out in the tragedy: we had to end the action in a suitable manner. It was a point I put up for grabs to the crew. Ton Kochen, the engineer, suggested we deliver the text of the British resolution to each skipper in the whaling fleet. Naoko translated it. We would deliver the message in suitable containers by helicopter in the morning as our parting gesture of protest.

Henk had the bright idea of lightening up the event by cooking some whale-shaped biscuits to accompany the text with a note saying, 'If you want to eat whales, eat these!' I retreated to the sanctuary of my cabin while the galley got to work and Naoko translated in the radio room.

The delivery run went off fine the next morning, and we left the ship we had shadowed for so long to resume our voyage. I had just finished putting out the final press release and pictures when I noticed a pile of papers close by Naoko's arm. They looked like the texts we thought we had delivered to the whalers.

'Naoko, please do not. . . . DO NOT tell me that all we put in the containers were biscuits?'

She looked at them uncomprehendingly, then her face flushed and she rushed out of the radio room. I buried my head in my hands and moaned loudly. We had been underway for five hours, but there was no alternative to the course of action we must take. I wearily climbed the stairs to the bridge.

'Arne, I'm afraid that if it's OK with you, we need to turn right around and find the whaling fleet again.'

'Are we going to give them hell again, Wilks?' he asked innocently.

I slumped onto the day-bunk. 'I am deeply embarrassed to tell you that what we delivered to the whaling fleet a few hours ago were a few whale-shaped biscuits. The texts of the resolution are still on board. We forgot to put them in the containers. Anyone on the bridge who laughs will be thrown over the side.'

Everyone creased up with laughter and soon I too was giggling at the ridiculousness of the situation. Between guffaws, Arne said, 'Bring her round.'

We found the fleet without problems and I explained what had happened to the Nishin Maru's skipper. I could feel the grin on his face through the radio set, but he graciously allowed us to complete our task, and Dave Walley went aloft again in the chopper.

I speculated at the cost to Greenpeace in terms of helicopter fuel and ship's diesel of delivering these messages which would, in all likelihood, be binned without being read. This was one story we wouldn't tell the press. I knew Paul Brown would keep it under his hat. I went down to the radio room to Naoko who had received the rough edge of my tongue earlier. She was in tears and looked up with reddened eyes and whispered, 'I so solly, Peter.' I gave her a big hug and said I was solly too, and soon we were laughing helplessly. The release of tension after the extraordinary events of the past ten days was sweet.

Our anti-whaling excursion had catapulted the expedition onto the world's front pages once again, and we set off happily on the four day journey towards World Park Base at Cape Evans, Ross Island. There we would carry out the resupply and undertake our last action, against the Americans at McMurdo Sound.

17. McMurdo

In the haven of my cabin, I cranked up the music and sang loudly in exhilaration. I looked at my wall chart on the bulkhead, showing the 'events' we had to perform before the trip was over. Only two to go.

After a night trying to sleep through the crash and bang of ice against the hull, I came up for the watch to find Ken humming with energy and bonhommie, always a bad sign for me. Sure enough, hardly able to keep the grin off his face, he asked me to clean the bridge windows – from the outside. He took great delight, sitting in the skipper's chair, making jocular comments to others on the bridge and pointing out areas I had missed while I froze, teetering perilously on a tiny ledge and scraping away over an expanse of 20 feet.

As the glacier-topped Balleny Islands slipped astern, we scanned the horizon for other familiar landmarks of our southern journey. There was the shimmering vision of Mount Erebus, two miles high, visible from a hundred kilometres away. Then we were nudging the floes of the inner ice pack.

I felt as though I were returning home. I took the glasses and picked up the small smudge of green against the black volcanic soil and white ice. This was World Park Base, the biggest adventure Greenpeace had ever undertaken, and home to the friends we had left there, 12 months ago.

Within the hour we were amongst the winterers, hugging, slapping backs, tousling hair, talking, shouting and laughing, a melée of folk so pleased to be once again in each other's company after so long a separation. The winterers had erected a banner on the side of the base depicting a graceful minke whale with the legend, 'Thank you Greenpeace. From the whales.' Stupid and sentimental though it was, a lump appeared in my throat and I fought back tears.

The resupply was completed. Ken's boundless energy and professionalism made the operation go like clockwork. We delayed celebration until our final action was over – blocking the McMurdo pipeline.

The US base at McMurdo Sound looked for all the world as though someone had removed a Siberian gulag and dumped it in Antarctica.

Observation Hill, from where Scott's men had kept watch for the arrival of their relief ship, is scarred (as is the entire encampment) by the tracks of tyres and roadways. Giant oil tanks dot the landscape rising from the black, volcanic soil. Rows of dormitory buildings follow the contours of the land between which dusty roadways snake, constantly plied by construction vehicles, naval trucks and personnel carriers. Overhead, twice a day, huge C130 air transports drone to land on the 'blue ice' runway at Williams Field. The smooth line of the foreshore at first seems to be a neatly manicured apron of black top soil, but this on inspection turns out to be concealing thousands of tons of metallic rubbish in layered chaos which spills into the sea. Toxic wastes pour from a discharge pipe contaminating the once pristine waters. Winterquarters Bay is biologically dead. McMurdo is polluted and defiled. Yet if you stand with your back to this running sore, you see the majestic mountain ranges of Victorialand and a wilderness of unsurpassed beauty.

Ron LeCount, head of operations for the National Science Foundation who were responsible for the mess of Winterquarters Bay, looked like a New York cabbie with a hard, gruff exterior. Ron and I had crossed swords before, and he was well known to Dog in Washington. He seemed to think I was Irish, and often muttered the occasional obscene remark about 'that Irishman Wilkinson.' For all our opposing views, I had a soft spot for Ron and he for me, as though we were acting out parts when we met annually at the bottom of the world. When the cameras had gone and duty done, Ron relaxed into a kind, charming guy.

Paul Bogart was running this protest though, being American himself, and I thankfully took a back seat. A specially drafted US sheriff flew into McMurdo base as we arrived and told us pointedly that the base, under US law, was part of the United States. If carried out by a US national, blocking the pipeline would constitute a felony. If carried out by non-US nationals, those involved would also face arrest should they ever set foot in the States.

We altered plans amid acrimony and chaos, brought about by 20 different opinions from the crew as to the legitimacy of the US claim and how we should react to it. Finally we decided we could not block the pipe. Instead, we would partially fill 5-gallon drums with the waste and make token protest with it to the NFS.

I spent a day in the workshop on the Gondwana painting seven 55 gallon drums with letters that read: 'D-A-N-G-E-R! C-A-D-M-I-U-M'. We would use our small Kabota tractor to pull the trailer and barrels to the outfall pipe where we would half-fill them with liquid cadmium waste. After that we would take them to the NSF Chalet and drop a large banner from the roof of the chalet for the cameras. Then we would tow the barrels back to the ship and deliver them to the US embassy in Wellington with a request that the Americans dispose of the waste responsibly. The 'action' had turned into a demonstration in the face of the legal threat. The compromise was one I hoped the exhausted crew could live with.

It was a bitterly cold and windy morning. Ron LeCount was waiting for us as the Gondwana nudged alongside the ice wharf at McMurdo.

'You can get this piece of shit outta here, soon as you like, asshole,' he told me, nodding over my shoulder at the ship. 'And don't think,' he continued, 'you're gettin' away with some fool-crazy stunt that'll screw up operations. I was supposed to leave this god-awful place yesterday, so I'm pissed at you guys.'

I pulled out a hip flask and took a slug. 'Ron, if you're pissed at having to stay an extra day, think how pissed we and millions of people are that you've ruined this piece of Antarctica, which is as much my backyard as yours. And you Yanks can get this piece of shit' – I embraced the sprawling mess of McMurdo with a sweep of my arm – 'outta here, as soon as YOU like, asshole.'

'We understand each other. You guys have a safe trip. I'll be in London in May, Wilkinson, I'll look you up. We got your home number on file. See ya.'

We shook hands and he shuffled off to the warmth of his office. The temperature had dropped to -25°C. In the whipping wind, the effective temperature was -50°C, and moisture on beards froze immediately. The tractor would not start. Tempers and accusations flared irrationally and dangerously.

Everyone was on short fuse. Without the tractor we had no alternative but to haul the trailer with the empty barrels to the outfall pipe, a distance of 500 yards. Then we filled the barrels and struggled with the trailer, vastly heavier now, to the NSF Chalet 700 yards up a steep gradient. This was cruel work. As we sweated, so the sweat froze on our foreheads or trickled down inside our thermal clothing to form pools in our boots. Eventually, we had the barrels lined up in front of the Chalet and six people clambered on the roof to drop the banner. I thankfully slumped down in a hollow to get out of the wind while Paul did his stuff. Through a megaphone, he called on the NSF personnel to come and meet us to discuss, in front of cameras, the disgrace of the pollution in the Bay. Only the moaning wind returned his call. He laid into the NSF which had for 30 years allowed such contamination in and around the base. Paul's lips were freezing as he spoke and his speech became more and more slurred. The hood of his Parka slipped down over his eyes and his performance, while passionate and professionally delivered, assumed a Laurel and Hardy tone the longer he went on. Then it was over. I mentally struck off the final remaining mark on my 'events' counter in my cabin. I was ready for home. The sense of relief was enormous.

As we dismantled the trappings of the protest to take back to the ship, the Kabota came hurtling round the corner. Someone had managed to fix it. We hitched the trailer on, and loaded ourselves as well. As I bounced

It's over! Jubilant protesters head for the ship and home after the final protest during the 1988-89 trip to McMurdo Base. Wojtek Moscal drives, Albert Kuichen (mate) acts as counterbalance on the Kabota *(Steve Morgan)*.

along next to Paul, I grabbed him.

'Well done, Dog. All over! Just the party at the hut and we're outta here. Yippppeeee!!'

Back on board, Ron LeCount called to say his goodbyes. He had watched the entire demonstration and had a question for us.

'I always knew you were a crazy bunch, but why in hell did you pull the trailer UP the hill, and drive it DOWN?' Paul told him it was in the interests of energy conservation.

We left Cape Evans on the 24th February after a humdinger of a hooley. Before it started I formally thanked everyone for their patience and hard work on a long and exhausting trip. The 'key' of the hut (actually the tool used to open the fuel barrels) was officially handed over to its new residents of the morrow; we all shook hands and hugged; then the party began.

The Antarctic midnight sun streamed through the windows as Keith Swenson and I donned heavy clothing and walked out into the night. A penguin's cry could be heard skidding across the ice from three miles away. Only the gentle creak of moving ice-floes disturbed the exquisite tranquility. We wandered along the coastline for a few miles taking in this remarkable place, drinking in its opium of peace and grandeur.

Out in the Bay stood our sturdy little ship, a splash of red against the bulk of Mount Erebus thrusting upwards into the pure air. There was the sudden 'whhooosssshhhh' of a whale sounding close to the edge of the fast ice. I squirmed on my stomach to within feet of a group of Adelie penguins oblivious to my presence. Laying there, I said my last farewell to the place, and allowed my thoughts to wander to the return trip with all its hazards, to the now vast organisation of Greenpeace, and the new breed of executives who seemed to sit in the offices these days. Keith shook me from my reveries. 'Let's move out, Wilks, unless you're overwintering. We've a ship to catch.'

The final goodbyes to the wintering team, on board the following day, were as emotional as always. There were few dry eyes as the choppers lifted for their final run ashore. Then they were gone, and there was a tangible emptiness. Into that void stepped the winterers who had done their stint – good friends and good shipmates. I walked across to Bogart and we hugged each other mightily: 'You bastard, Wilks.' he said, 'I wouldn't have missed this for the world.'

Our easy ride home wasn't to be. A thousand miles from us, events were conspiring to ensure that Dog and I were as busy on the way back as we had been on the way down. The Bahia Pariso, an Argentinian Antarctic supply/passenger vessel, had gone aground in the peninsula region. Her grounding was closely followed by another. Newspaper hacks from around the world assumed that we must be somewhere near, still being in Antarctic waters ourselves. They wanted 'eye-witness accounts' and our opinions. We used this free platform to point out the dangers of transporting oil round polar regions, and to press home our case to the Antarctic Treaty Party nations, not to open up the continent to mining.

Later, the Exxon Valdiz was to go aground in Alaska, near the other pole. The awful folly of commercial oil extraction in polar regions was staring at the world.

So anxious were we to keep the media happy, that we fed them a second-hand story told to us by an 'eye witness' about jumping krill. Supposedly on the spot, he had reported that the krill were 'jumping' out of the oil-covered sea in an effort to stay alive. This was a very popular account and much repeated by the press. Unknown to us, biologists round the world laughed outright at the ridiculousness of this particular bit of Greenpeace nonsense, and Dog and I spent much time on our return good-naturedly blaming each other for using such a ridiculous quote.

As February gave way to March, Ken repeatedly tapped the barometer and said he'd never seen it fall so low. He issued orders to prepare for what he gleefully called 'the storm of the century'. All deadlights were to be fastened, cargo and helicopter lashings were doubly secured, and any loose material in the cabins and saloon tied firmly down.

As I tried to sleep that evening, the storm took hold of the ship. On watch the following day, the sight was something to behold. Great walls of water stood vertically, towering 30 feet high, before crashing down with a force which jarred the ship from stem to stern. These monsters were stacked up to the horizon in great serried ranks waiting to batter us; and we were still in waters which harboured growlers and small bergs. The Antarctic light failed at midnight, and Ken turned on the spotlight to aid us lookouts. The bridge was facing mounting chaos as charts slid from the chart table and drawers spilled their contents over the deckhead. From below came the sounds of splintering furniture, crashing glass and the curses of the crew.

As the ship reached the pinnacle of a wave, it held its breath for a second, hanging mid-air. Then the bow would free-fall through 30 feet to plunge with a shuddering blow into the solid floor of water below. Sleep was impossible, as one moment you were driven deep into your bunk by gravity and the next, suspended six inches above it.

We recorded wind gusts of 100 mph. During the two days it lasted, parts of the superstructure were torn away, but none of the damage was irreparable, nothing crucial missing. Crew appeared from their private hells like wraiths, wild-eyed, drawn and pale. I was delighted. The Southern Ocean had given me its very best display as I left it for the last time.

Now nothing stood between us and home. Temperatures began to rise. Soon we could smell the sweet aroma of vegetation one hundred miles from land. And I took my last full watch of the trip, watching lights along the New Zealand coast twinkle as we slid by them. Ken and I shook hands after the watch, downed a few beers and then walloped the rum mercilessly. Tomorrow we would face the press, a Maori welcome and the rigours of adjusting, once again, to a normal life.

18. Behaving Badly

Every year since we had set up the base, the pattern would be the same. I would get home full of relief, determined never to go near the place again. On the Antarctic expeditions we lived on adrenaline and played hard, but also worked to the limits of endurance. Emotions were constantly volatile in those days without night, and it was my overall responsibility to keep everyone functioning well and meet campaign objectives; to ensure we succeeded in the face of terrible conditions. I was frequently seasick, homesick, and near permanently exhausted. Every year I would spend a couple of months after returning from the Antarctic mooching around, picking up a little freelance work here and there. Then a call would come from Greenpeace, and I would find myself preparing to go back again.

Every year, when I got home, I found it harder to identify with changes in the Greenpeace organisation and found I disagreed with much of its new ethos. I felt it had lost direction: something recognised within the ranks of Greenpeace itself. In 1987 I had written an article in a leading New Zealand newspaper which asked Greenpeace to look at its operation in a self-analytical manner. Open criticism was frowned upon, and invariably caused a closing of ranks within the broad organisation. It was an attitude I found hard to accept. Worse, I was no longer very welcome around Greenpeace personnel. I was tolerated – as long as I was sufficiently far away from the hub of the empire and sufficiently preoccupied so as not to present too much of a problem. But I was ignored when back in the UK.

My anger festered over several years, and overspilled shortly after our return from that extraordinary fourth trip. We were celebrating in a restaurant in Auckland, wrapped in the usual bonhomie which enveloped the crews after a long and difficult voyage.

Sitting waiting for us in the restaurant was someone whose face was familiar but whom I couldn't immediately place. Leather jacket, smartly creased trousers, fancy briefcase, mobile phone, scrubbed face, expensive haircut. I'd worked with him ten years before, and now we talked about the metamorphosis Greenpeace appeared to be going through. It was clear we were on different wavelengths. As the evening wore on, I told the poor bloke he was the unacceptable face of Greenpeace, and represented everything the organisation had become which was bad, cancerous and negative.

Surrounded by people whose history in Greenpeace had been bonded by a decade of common struggle against unequal odds, my sense of sacrifice and camaraderie felt invaded by this person. It was a bilious and unwarranted attack. He stalked out of the bar. To my shame, I recall shouting at his retreating figure to go back to the UK, get a real job and stop poncing on the efforts of others. I was getting seriously out of order. Worse, I couldn't walk away from the organisation with dignity.

Later that same evening, still full of landfall-bonhomie and even fuller of ice-cold New Zealand beer, we stood in yet another bar waiting to play pool.

In walked firstly Peter Melchett, executive director of Greenpeace UK, my replacement in 1986. In tow was Colin Hines, who had been working for Greenpeace for a year or so. Both were on fact-finding missions in the southern hemisphere. Colin had his wife and baby in tow, and I choked on my beer as I recalled the impossibility of toting my family round the world when we struggled from week to week to raise sufficient funds to finance the Warrior on the trips which had built Greenpeace.

Uncharitable was not the word to describe the mood I was in the following morning, and I found myself staring at the waters of Auckland Harbour over the gun'l of the ship, pondering my future and my attitude. Neither was healthy. I commanded respect with campaigners and crews, but was increasingly isolated and shunned by the hierarchy. I was bitter at my rejection. And I felt that the years of personal sacrifice and work had spawned an organisation which was in danger of losing its way.

Greenpeace employees now walked into a ready-made, viable and respected organisation. In the early days, to work for the organisation put you on the radical fringes of society and almost guaranteed that you would never be employed by a government agency or 'straight' employer. Latter-day Greenpeacers, on the contrary, could find their employment a test bed for a career in politics or the world of international agencies. The organisation was rapidly becoming part of the comfortable furniture of society, and respectable. These were not, in my opinion, attributes which would fire public imagination to the fever pitch necessary for an environmental revolution.

Greenpeace had in many respects become a victim of its own success. The public, politicians and industry now accepted the need for environmental reforms, and the media were tiring of the same old direct actions. Traditional targets were disappearing and new ones such as ozone depletion, global warming and deforestation were emerging as priorities. These were harder issues to tackle with a fleet of six or seven ships. The adversarial approach still characterised Greenpeace, when increasingly constructive and co-operative solutions seemed necessary, along with a new sort of radicalism. But now Greenpeace had millions to lose should radicalism bring it into conflict with the courts, and this tempers the attitudes of the decision-makers.

I dragged my gaze away from the glittering waters of Auckland Harbour and wended my way to my cabin. I whacked on some loud Hendrix and wrote to McTaggart.

Dear David,

My position in Greenpeace is unclear and it appears that after being fired in '86 from the board of Greenpeace UK, I have been employed as a consultant/employee of Greenpeace International to lead the Antarctic expeditions. It is clear I will never command any position which brings me back into the decision making fold, as my ideas are either too radical on the direct action front, or too uncomfortable.

When we spoke recently, you asked what I would do as an emergency package to contain and redirect Greenpeace. Having thought carefully, I offer the following advice:

Sack 50% of staff, drop 50% of campaigns and put a ceiling on salaries of $20,000 a year.

Clearly this will be unnacceptable, so I think the best thing is for me to formalise my departure. I hereby resign and let you know I will be unavailable for any future expeditions or campaigns which take me away from the UK for any length of time.

I read and re-read my words. So many years of slog, pain, elation and adventure over and done with. Just the round of good-byes, while most other crew were already talking about next year's expedition, and then the journey home.

After that fourth trip, Paul 'Doglips' Bogart moved to International to take over the entire Antarctic campaign co-ordination. He wanted continuity on the expeditions and invited applications for a three year post of ship-based co-ordinator. I wasn't prepared to give such a long term commitment, and the position I had held for four consecutive expeditions went to someone else.

But that summer, back in London, the Antarctic call still came. Paul asked if I would act as adviser to the fifth expedition. Although I wouldn't be making the trip, I would have the chance to spend another northern winter in the heat of New Zealand. New Zealand in November is a wonderful place. Late spring is giving way to early summer. The atmosphere in Auckland is gay and carefree. And living on a ship in the centre of town, the stream of friends and visitors is constant. Invitations to parties, beach excursions and trips to the bush are endless. The temptation was too great, and I arrived to proffer my advice to the new kid on the block,

American Dana Harman, a short, energetic and determined woman.

When the ship pulled away from the quayside to sail south once again, I could barely contain my tears. There they went, Ken, Werner, Arne, Marc, Keith, Sabine and lots of other friends with whom I had shared so many experiences, leaving port without me. Their departure left a void. Alcohol failed to numb my sense of loss.

I arrived home in January after a holiday. The Gulf War was about to begin. England was depressing, cold and miserable.

I resumed work as an independent consultant. Greenpeace UK was situated just a couple of miles from where I sat at my computer day in, day out, trying to drum up work. Peter Melchett, still Chair at GPUK told a confidant of his that under different circumstances, he would not have hesitated to hire me, as I was considered the 'best campaigner around'.

I did pick up work, carrying out speaking engagements, consultancy work for Greenpeace International and for a green bathroom toiletries group, Montagne Jeunesse. I was editor and author of the Ideal Home's 'Greener Home' exhibition brochure, and made all sorts of contacts which

Memories from happier times . . . (left to right) Sabine Schmidt, Keith Swenson and Pete Wilkinson take time out in the Apple survival hut after a hard day's monitoring at McMurdo (Tim Baker).

could have stood me in good stead had I not been continually gnawed by the Antarctic bug. I couldn't settle.

It's difficult to describe the intensity of the adrenaline boost my system was used to receiving each year, and the state of barely containable excitement I always experienced before leaving. As each British summer waned and the nights drew in, my body began to itch for movement away. I often found myself seeking out the southern sector of the sky, like a bird preparing to migrate. I slept restlessly, paced endlessly.

During the summer of 1990, Doglips called from Washington. Would I lead a team on the 90/91 expedition, to camp out at McMurdo for a month with the winterers? The job was to monitor the environmental 'clean up' the US Government had announced.

Then he dropped a bombshell.

Greenpeace were pulling World Park Base out of the Antarctic. It had served its purpose. To everyone's great delight and surprise, the Antarctic Treaty Nations had finally agreed to a 50-year moratorium on mining. The grounding of two ships in the region the previous summer, followed by the Exxon Valdiz catastrophe in the Arctic, had reinforced the arguments we had been putting forward for years and (perversely) helped the conservation cause enormously. Our campaign and McTaggart's vision had paved the way.

Dana Harmon was to be the expedition co-ordinator again; it would be the first time I'd been on an Antarctic voyage without being 'in charge'. The prospect did not excite me, but if I wanted to go south, here was my chance. I prevaricated for weeks, though my decision was inevitable.

As I was preparing to leave once again, the Greenpeace lawyer, Sarah Burton, phoned. During a company restructuring, she said, it had been discovered that there was reason to believe the share I was issued in 1978 was still valid.

In order to 'finally set the records straight', my signature was required on a retroactive resolution. Signature on a share transfer form would be required too. After all this time, it seemed I still did have a share. I was intrigued.

I met Sarah in Islington and asked her to translate the five or six pages of legalese into plain English. The resolution appeared to me to approve retroactively all decisions made by the board over the past five years. I wanted to be sure of the full consequences of signing, and said I would discuss the matter with my own lawyer, leaving the meeting with a wry smile on my face. However much Greenpeace UK ignored me, I still had a legal interest.

A few phone calls later, it was apparent the resolution was a serious matter. Matti Wuori, the newly appointed Chairman of Greenpeace International, called to say he would appreciate it if I signed quickly. Unless I did so, the individuals on the Greenpeace board in London risked heavy financial penalties and many of the current campaigns would be in jeopardy. I couldn't make sense of it. No-one seemed willing to explain, other than in legal jargon, quite why this was so or why the situation had arisen. I still refused to sign until I was clear what I was signing. Matti said he would come to London to discuss it. This WAS serious.

At dinner with Matti, he was equally vague as to why my signature was so urgently needed and repeated what he'd said on the phone. Unless the resolution was signed by all shareholders and directors, the international campaign programme was at risk. But when pressed as to exactly why, Matti would only answer 'it was complicated'.

I felt uneasy about this urgency and wasn't about to sign away any influence I might still be able to exert over the future of Greenpeace. Since I was, after all, a shareholder, and had not, whether by oversight or design, been invited to any Annual General Meetings since 1986, nor had been advised about the issuing of further shares, I felt the least I could expect was an explanation in unequivocal terms. I declined to sign.

As October approached I prepared to leave for New Zealand, anxiously awaiting the arrival of my contract for the trip. I was only weeks from leaving for six months, travelling to the ends of the earth. We had verbally agreed terms, at which time Paul had said the fee I had asked was well below the equivalent of the salary a senior campaigner was currently making. When the contract still failed to arrive, I called Dog in desperation, to find out what the hold-up was. He told me he had been advised not to send it until I signed the resolution from the UK board. And he risked his job telling me.

Although McTaggart had not been involved in any of these goings-on, I called him and spilled out my bile. He was sympathetic but non-commital, suggesting I work it out in my own way.

The executive director of Greenpeace International, Steve Sawyer, then entered the fray to do some sorting. I remembered Steve arriving in London back in the 70s. He was a typical 'greenie': long hair swept back in a pony-tail, softly spoken and with an intensity about him which marked him for greater things even then. We took him under our wing in the UK office, finding him a place to crash and occupying him on various tasks, one of which was to help in the direct actions in Barrow. He and I had been in the same inflatable dinghy, singing 'We shall not be moved' at the top of our voices waiting to be crushed against a quayside. Now Steve was probably the most powerful person in the organisation and had come to the UK to trouble-shoot this little problem.

In the face of Steve's reassuring presence and reasonable tone, my obstinacy waned. Everyone else had signed. It suddenly seemed a trifling matter. I wanted to conclude this amicably and I didn't want there to be any lasting bad blood between me and the UK office; I hoped for freelance work from them. And I also wanted to go to the Antarctic very badly.

There were two other things I wanted. One of them I knew would be dismissed out of hand. The other would not have gone amiss during my own days on the board and I had put much serious thought into it. I decided this would be the price of my signature on that document.

'So what do you want, Wilks?' Steve enquired.

'I want £200,000 to run a campaign against Sellafield.'

'Oh yeah, sure! What do you really want?'

'I want the UK board to be answerable to an electoral college which would review all decisions and take an advisory role. One third of the college would be drawn from the ranks of people without whom Greenpeace would not exist today, including me. Those people have a right to have their voices heard.'

To my surprise, Steve readily agreed to this. He returned to the UK a few days later to sign a letter of agreement, and the necessary papers, at the offices of my lawyer. At the meeting, we had before us a document containing all the names I wanted to see on the electoral college. It also contained the procedural arrangements: appointment of members before December 1991, and the first election of the board by June 1992. I charged Steve for my time, and my legal fees came to £4,600. The cheque, the signatures and the letter of agreement were exchanged in late October. I went for a beer with Steve and chewed over old times before he grabbed his bag and headed off to Amsterdam. I was content with the arrangement we had made. The UK Board would be answerable at last to a truly representative electoral college.

19. Where's the Action Section?

By the time we left Auckland on the trip to pull the base out, I had decided I would keep out of Dana Harman's way as much as possible. My initial enthusiasm for her abilities had waned quickly. She was affable and conversational when socialising, but when it came to the expedition and work I found her distant. I tried to keep reminding myself she was in a difficult position, and clearly did not want to be beholden to me, or indeed any, of the experienced people on board. She needed to carve her own style and stamp her own brand of authority. Even so, I found it difficult to be gracious and began to stay in my cabin during crew meetings.

I felt desperately homesick during the voyage, and knew I needed to plan some sort of alternative, non-Greenpeace career. I also had to begin learning to live in one place again. I mused that I would soon be asked to sit on the Greenpeace UK electoral college and even, perhaps, be invited to serve a term on the board from which my colleagues and I had so casually and stupidly resigned in 1986.

Greenpeace was officially leaving Antarctica after achieving the most outstanding campaign success in its history, and the most significant green victory to date. Many of us 'Vets' wanted to celebrate the salvation of the continent in an appropriate manner, once the base was dismantled. I suggested a Greenpeace mini-expedition across the ice-shelf to Scott's last resting place, climbing a hitherto unconquered peak in the Transantarctic range in the company of Chris Bonnington, a foray around Ross Island and this wonderland we had rescued. But none of these ideas was taken up.

Before we could draw breath after the work was finished, the ship was made ready for immediate departure. Ken arrived at my door waving a bottle of whisky. We were leaving Cape Evans for the very last time and he wanted to celebrate, even if Dana didn't. I was surprised and hurt that she hadn't thought to tell me of the departure.

My last memory of the place was watching it disappear behind the helideck of the Gondwana, as Ken and I huddled under a blanket. We drank quickly and urgently, hands freezing as we risked a slurp of whisky from our icy tumblers. Our silences became longer, and we receded into private memories of unsurpassable adventures. It seemed to me, and I guess to him, to have been a lifetime of commitment to a place which had sucked our souls dry at times, and taken us to the very limits of human emotion and experience.

It was a difficult voyage for me most of the way, and I ached to reach Auckland. I had planned to stay two weeks to help Ken with discharging the ship. Once back in town, though, I was overwhelmed by the need to get home immediately.

Arriving in London, I called Steve Sawyer to see what progress had been made. He was 'out'. After a few days of badgering, I received a message to say I would be informed of the situation 'as soon as possible'. Time passed and I heard nothing. I rang a few people I had listed for the electoral college. Only one had been approached – Tony Marriner, a long serving employee who was still heading up the Communications Division. He had said yes, but then heard nothing.

I eventually found out that a small electoral college was being put in place at Greenpeace UK, and was indeed being instituted in all Greenpeace offices. However, the agreement had called for the college to be installed by December 31st. It was now March and, so far, not one name on my list had been appointed.

While I anxiously waited and quietly fumed, others were accusing Greenpeace UK of isolationism and loss of direction. Paul Brown, the *Guardian* newspaper journalist, took these criticisms, including my beef about the electoral college, to Peter Melchett (the executive director) at a lunch appointment. Melchett's response to the electoral college question was that, as a former employee, I was not in a position to dictate the complexion of the electoral college and had no rights in the matter.

The whole deal had become a confused mess. The agreement I thought I had secured through Steve Sawyer seemed either to have been reinterpreted, or had not constitued a valid agreement at all, despite the careful and expensive paperwork. All the time I had been away, I had had visions of approaches being made to all the old stalwarts of the organisation to help Greenpeace move into the 1990s. I felt drained and used and full of pain.

There was clearly no room within the organisation for me, although I was still being offered positions working for the international body, now settled in Amsterdam. These jobs were invariably of long duration, and tended to be in places a long way away from home – like joining the office in Kiev, for instance. If I was seriously to carve an alternative career for myself, or ever have a satisfactory personal life, I knew it had to be in London.

I tried to put Greenpeace out of my mind, and retired to lick my wounds. I began acting as consultant to Wide Open Communications who were involved in exhibiting a 'green' home at the Ideal Home Exhibition in London. David Bellamy and I addressed assembled dignitaries at the opening of the house, and later sat on a panel of experts to judge various entries for the Green Awards. I was then seconded to the Trustee Saving Bank Environmental Investment Fund, of which David was the chairman. As our paths crossed more and more frequently, I began to get an insight into this man of boundless energy. David has undoubtedly popularised 'the environment' more than any other single person around. His endearing antics on television capture the attention of millions, while his ability to explain the convoluted workings of the biosphere in an entertaining and understandable way has contributed more to encouraging sympathy and support for the green movement than all the campaigns of Greenpeace and Friends of the Earth combined. He is rare. He is not averse to putting his own not-inconsiderable bulk on the picket line when necessary, as he did in the Gordon River Dam campaign in Tasmania some years ago. I had first come across him first many years before, during a campaign in Billingham, Teeside, where we helped the local community fight off the plans of NIREX (Nuclear Industry Radioactive Waste Executive) to use a disused ICI plant as a nuclear dump.

David is somewhat set apart from the mainstream green movement in the UK, whatever that is defined as these days. He has his own agenda, and spends much of his time moving round the world. I had long felt that if I could pin him down and get the other personalities of the green movement together for long enough and set them down working on a clear, concise and focused agenda, we could actually get somewhere. On my return from New Zealand, it had taken me a few weeks to get a handle on what the green movement was up to in the UK, so long had been my absence. The scene was flat. Nothing appeared to be going on. It was most depressing. Mrs Thatcher had pulled the rug from beneath the feet of the greens by her 'we are all green now' speech to the UN, and everyone was staring at each other, saying 'What now?'

I thought it was time to get some of the luminaries together to set an agenda. I had a few ideas I wanted to float. I set about the daunting task of trying to get them in the same place at the same time, an exercise which took three months.

I invited Graham Searle (founder of Friends of the Earth in the UK), David Bellamy, Jonathan Porritt, Teddy Goldsmith (founder of the *Ecologist* Magazine and veteran green campaigner), Bryn Jones, Reg Boorer, David Gee (then director of Friends of the Earth) and Peter Melchett (executive director of Greenpeace).

Getting these guys together ranked as a minor miracle. In the end David Gee and Peter Melchett were unable to attend. But the rest of us met in the Island Queen pub in Islington in the summer of 1991, and a plan of sorts began to emerge over a series of meetings which followed. We would target the upcoming general election, thought to be scheduled for November, and we would force the environment back onto the agenda through a series of hard-hitting advertisements which would pinpoint the ten most pressing issues and their solutions, couched so simply it would 'convince your granny', as Reg put it.

I wrote and circulated the first draft for comment. The corrections, while improving the accuracy, had the inevitable effect of lengthening the copy to the point of unwieldiness. I felt we still had a product, and we pressed ahead. It was also our intention to canvas the views of all prospective Parliamentary candidates on these same ten issues.

A head of steam built up and, at the fourth meeting, Reg brought in an advertising team with whom he had worked on other projects, who gave us invaluable advice over the months and charged us nothing. They suggested a countdown technique to be launched 12 days before the general election. A series of obscure ads would get the public guessing what was coming. With each day's ad, more would become clear until, on the last day, two days before the election, we would publish the results of the survey and blatantly tell people not to vote for those politicians who responded negatively.

I was very excited by the project, but my excitement was tempered by the near impossibility of raising the funds – an estimated £250,000. I had known all along we might have a tough time convincing these guys that finding and spending that sort of money would be worth it, but I had a certain amount of optimism. After all, they'd come this far on the project. There was a shuffling of feet and a scraping of chairs when the sum was mentioned.

Teddy Goldsmith suddenly expressed his doubts. He said we were trying to sell the environment as if we were selling toothpaste. Reg said, 'Yup, that's exactly what we want to do.'

Jonathan then expressed reservations along the same lines. Pretty soon it was clear that raising the money with the help of those assembled was unlikely. We left agreeing to proffer our thoughts by letter over the coming few weeks, but as I walked from the room, a great void opened. I glanced at Reg. He shrugged as if to say, 'What do you expect?' The idea died a reasonably peaceful death and the environment as an issue was nowhere on the agenda when the General Election came round.

I surveyed the horizons of the green movement searching for the daring, imagination and political vision associated with achieving results of national or global significance. My optimism and energies waned.

We had achieved unprecedented acceptance of green issues; universal recognition of the serious and inescapable problems we had to face up to. Green organisations had never had so much money, so much profile or so much going for them, yet for some reason they were not using this strength to forge a radical green agenda. Had I dreamt back in the 1970s that we would be in this position by the early 1990s, I would have predicted that the necessary conditions for a true green revolution were in place. It was now clear that I would have been wrong.

Knowing my time wasn't being used to the full, my old friend and fellow board member, Reg Boorer, called me in March 1992. He'd been approached by a public relations agency in Hamburg which had a major multi-national client who were looking for a 'big environmental idea' to further boost their corporate image. Reg asked me to think about it, and also brought in Gerry Matthews, an ex-researcher from FoE. We hit on suggesting to the company that they become 'guardians of the world's water', encouraging their millions of customers to become 'water misers'. To put these proposals in an acceptable package, we had to create a name for ourselves. For the sake of efficiency, we called ourselves WBM – Wilkinson, Boorer, Matthews – and added 'Environmental Communications'.

As a team, we were full of energy and ideas, and shared the belief that a fresh tack should be adopted in addressing green issues. We had other ideas and began to think big. WBM intended to encourage industry to grasp the environmental nettle in an imaginative and visionary manner. We would help companies seize the initiative and plan for sustainable development.

I was still independently consumed with Sellafield, however, and hatched a direct action plan to stop the commissioning of the Thermal Oxide Reprocessing Plant (THORP), which I would put into operation at the opportune time. I needed to know if I was still bound by the injunctions I had been served in the 1980s, and wrote to Sarah Burton at Greenpeace to ask if she would send copies of any outstanding legal hangovers. I could not resist having a dig at her in the letter:

'I hope you are happy with the outcome of the electoral college issue.'

She phoned next morning. I had assumed she might be a little defensive but instead she was angry. The agreement I had made, she said, had been with Steve Sawyer not with Greenpeace UK, and it was not binding on the UK office.

I couldn't believe Steve could have treated me contemptuously. I was devastated by the misunderstandings, and plunged into depression. I seemed to be, once again, out in the cold.

The stark choice I had to make was either to battle on to sort out the confusion using the documents Sawyer had signed, or to recognise and accept that the 15 years I had been associated with the organisation were over.

I decided to break the cord. It was intensely painful, like being weaned off a drug, like being separated from your family, like being banished to bleak hills from where you could only look down on the vitality and activity going on in a town below.

In 1987, Fred Pearce wrote a book called *Green Warriors*. It accurately relates the manner in which the first faltering steps of Friends of the Earth gave way to the Rolls Royce of Greenpeace in the 1980s. Everyone is there: 'guru' Teddy Goldsmith, Professor David Bellamy, Jonathan Porritt, Bryn Jones, yours truly and a score of others round the world, most notably Petra Kelly, who did more for the green cause than most of us put together.

The green movement today, Fred Pearce's homage notwithstanding, has faced a difficult time since his book was written. Some would say it has been neutered. It is certainly less radical.

I needed something which would restore my faith. The Rio Earth Summit beckoned. I harboured reservations about the ability of the greens to rise to the occasion, I even doubted that we were a 'movement' as such: merely disparate individuals and groups taking opportunities to promote ideas and campaigns as they arose, rather than a cohesive, homogenous body moving forward in unison. But I lived in hope that the gathering of Heads of State would provide a landmark in ecological reforms. We all did.

Jonathan Porritt launched his book, *Save the Earth* prior to Rio. He had been attacked in the *Independent* that morning for producing another glossy, expensive coffee-table book preaching its message to the converted. Jonathan, always an impressive orator, delivered a withering defense of what he'd written, before getting down to the business in hand – the Earth Summit. He spoke well and convincingly about its importance and then turned to his piéce de resistance, the 'action section'.

It was a 'Tree of Life': a papiér maché tree onto which would be stuck all the 'leaves' people would send from around the world to Jonathan in Rio. These 'leaves' were to be found in the book which was already in great demand in over 20 countries. As a public relations exercise it was a winner, but as an example of late 20th century campaigning pressure on international governments it left me despairing. Had we done so much, come so far, and risked everything, to have the focus on Rio reduced to a papiér maché tree sprouting paper leaves ?

Nevertheless Jonathan, when it came to it, achieved more than most in Rio to push for adherence to a radical agenda which might belatedly begin to address the immense, though not insoluble problems of global starvation, climate change, ozone layer depletion, poverty and disease.

Up on Sugar Loaf Mountain, Greenpeace hung a banner with a picture of the Earth and a sign:

'Sold'

A tidal wave of dejection swamped over me. In this mood of crushing negativity all I could see were comfortable images, comfortable demonstrations, comfortable pressure which politicians and custodians of the planet could rub against in the knowledge that little would be demanded of them: sincere, controllable protest, which allowed everyone to convince themselves that things would get better simply by discussing the issues.

But then, I asked myself, what was *I* doing to pin our world leaders to the wall ?

Sold? The Greenpeace banner on Sugar Loaf Mountain at the Rio Earth Summit. A lot of effort for only modest returns *(Morgan/Greenpeace)*.

20. Olive Branch

All the cataclysmic impacts of environmental decline – rising sea levels, melting ice caps, massive increases in skin cancers, fundamental shifts in weather patterns, crop failures and population explosions – are predicted to peak in the middle of the next century. A quantum leap in thought and action is due. Unless there is a polarisation of the stick-and-carrot approach of the green movement, unless we bring about serious and far-reaching changes within the next decade or two, we will have no movement to wring our hands over. It will be remembered as a predominantly white, western, middle class indulgence. Greenpeace, with its high profile, its notoriety and wealth and its continuing ability to be a royal pain in the butt to governments and industry round the world, must enter a new period of progressive and radical activity with flair and imagination and sheer brassneck. No other organisation has the resource-base, the flexibility or the power. Greenpeace must be seen to set the agenda, with clear goals in a set time frame, and continue to kick arse mercilessly when industry doesn't respond.

It must also speed up its decision-making process, which has become labyrinthine. Many activists are increasingly confused about its goals, strategies and tactics, and are becoming vocal in their frustration. A measure of this frustration was the recent seizing of the ageing ship, Sirius, by former crew members to prevent it from becoming a museum. They wanted to use it in direct actions to address reprocessing at Sellafield and Norwegian whaling. Greenpeace directors read the riot act to the protesters, persuaded them back to port, and re-took the ship.

Where the organisation succeeds, it succeeds well. Certain sectors are beginning to co-operate effectively with industry, despite a historical cynicism. And it's a highly impressive organisation. It has offices in over 30 countries with an income of tens of millions of dollars a year, and employs hundreds of people around the globe. Activists still take enormous risks. And the much needed rationalisation process is underway. In the USA alone, a 50% cut in staff has been painfully carried out, and throughout the empire, changes have forced a healthy shake-up. McTaggart resigned long ago, but had been brought back in the role of Honorary Chairman.

Greenpeace in Germany published an entire alternative edition of *Stern* magazine on chlorine-free paper to demonstrate that the difference in product quality and consumer appeal was unnoticeable. Greenpeace Sweden convinced IKEA, whose yearly catalogue devours 30,000 tones of pulp, to likewise refrain from using chlorine. In an inspired move, Greenpeace developed a CFC-free fridge and pumped money into a German factory to help it begin production.

These ideas are the 'direct actions of the 21st century'. They need to be expanded and explored, and very fast. In my wildest dreams, I see the green movement across the globe offering an olive branch to its traditional adversaries in industry, on a scale which sets the world alight with its novelty, which is irresistible in its vision and breathtaking in its audacity. One of these days, ICI or another such multinational conglomerate will be encouraged to make such a quantum leap forward. It will shake the world with a plan to pave the way for corporate husbandry of the planet in a manner which governments seem incapable of. The greening of our deserts, the provision of food for our starving on a truly massive scale, the voluntary global withdrawing of harmful chemical production, the buying up of our tropical forests and the provision of funds for their sustainable management, the adoption of the guardianship of our water, air and soil – all these things are possible should flexible and responsible multinationals be persuaded that they should be carried out for the sake of all our futures.

As WBM laboured through the end of 1992, awash with practical ideas but devoid of finance, we found we were positioning ourselves as a convenient bridging agent to industry. We were uniquely placed to act as facilitators and communicators: we knew the movement and its players, we knew the issues and, between the partners, we had contacts throughout the world. Moreover, we had all moved around outside the movement, dealing with advertising agencies, public relations companies, trades unions, university departments, the media, marketing and specialist organisations. We had credibility and, between us and our network of contacts, we also had the necessary range of skills which were both attractive to the industrial sector, and acknowledged by the greens.

It was only a matter of time, we repeatedly told ourselves, before the money followed the energy. And we had one thing going for us in a big way: the ideas we came up with were often towering, glittering mountains of ideas worthy of a sharp intake of breath.

Dave Gee, the ex-Director of Friends of the Earth, joined us, requiring a name change to WBMG. He continued to lecture and worked on a TV series about local environmental issues; Reg kept himself buoyant with his graphic designing skills; Gerry Matthews survived through his consultancy work and lecturing. I had a few small clients and earned enough to remain barely solvent month to month. Thankfully, I had one invaluable safety line – a lump-sum pension of £15,000 suggested by McTaggart back in 1986, to bring Greenpeace into line with normal employment practice. It was theoretically available to anyone who'd worked consistently for the organisation over ten years. And by the end of 1992, the money was nearly gone.

It was clear, as WBMG began to make more contacts, that the wounds inflicted during my battles with Greenpeace over the past six or seven years would have to be healed. At a Christmas bash in Fleet Street hosted by environmental journalists, I met up with Peter Melchett, Alan Thornton and the new kid on the Greenpeace block, Chris Rose. Peter expressed hopes that we could put differences behind us and enter a more productive phase. While I remained healthily sceptical about many aspects of the Greenpeace operation, I had to give him respect for taking the infant I had helped to bring into the world, – and doing a not-half bad job of seeing it through adolescence. We officially buried the hatchet with lunch and a handshake.

As 1992 slipped into 1993, some of the WBMG projects began to bear fruit. Contracts were signed. We were up and running.

McTaggart flew to England on one of his rare visits. We met over a traditional English dinner. I felt easy in the company of this magnetic man who had so fundamentally influenced my life. I had, and still have, an abiding affection for him and for a relationship based on mutual respect for what we had each individually faced and managed to do in our lives.

I told him about a Channel 4 documentary I'd been asked to research. It was to look at the dilemmas Greenpeace currently faces, and investigate how a bunch of idealistic, long-haired hippies had managed over the years to construct an internationally renowned and wealthy environmental organisation. As we mopped up the gravy on our plates and the beer flowed, David reviewed the chequered history of the organisation which still coursed through his veins, as it did mine.

I asked him what he considered his most serious mistakes, during 20 years steering Greenpeace. He sucked on his pint and averted his eyes; a mannerism which always preceded rare insight into the McTaggart soul.

'You have to understand, if I made one correct decision in ten, I mean CORRECT, I was doin' OK. But. . . .' he dumped his napkin, 'just for the record. I think I made a big mistake not getting you invited back on the UK board. Ha!'

I gestured to him with a flicker of fingers. 'Come on, David. Tell me, tell me.'

'Well, I realised you guys were gettin' outta line and had to go.'

'Over the fur campaign, right?'

'The fur campaign was nothin' – NOTHIN'! Jeez, you guys had a

Marxist as Chairman. You were sucking up to the unions at every turn and you, I remember, wanted to run for Labour Party nomination, for Chrissake. You guys were to the left of Engels. It was starting to be noticed. We couldn't have a major office going political on us. You had to go.'

I let the words sink in. Since 1986, I had believed – as I assumed did the rest of the organisation – that we had been ousted because of a campaign which compromised the Greenpeace empire on a point of political correctnesss. Although I disagreed with the decisions, I had respected them as corporate policy. To be told, six years on, that a false and eminently refutable myth had precipitated our removal, struck me as the ultimate irony.

Through tears of laughter and hopelessness, I looked McTaggart in the eye.

'You're so full of shit, David. I honestly don't know whether I'm laughing or crying. You got the important decisions right, sure. And I doff my cap to your intuition. But when you misread a situation, you really go big!

'What do you want to drink, asshole?'

End

I wonder, in my worst moments, if all the changes we invest our hopes in are indeed 'green-wash'; a good public relations exercise to sell a product better. Other times I do believe a sea change is underway. Who can tell?

Perhaps, in the last split-second of biological time, it will be recognised that some of our number stood up to be counted.

"OK Ingelnuk, make sure you catch him looking really fierce"

Satire that backfired: the offending *Greenpeace News* cartoon which accompanied an item apologising to supporters for pulling out of the anti-fur campaign to placate native peoples (see p.58) *(Richard Willson)*.

Index